WHY
BOWIE
MATTERS

WHY
BOWIE
MATTERS

WILL BROOKER

WILLIAM
COLLINS

William Collins
An imprint of HarperCollins*Publishers*
1 London Bridge Street
London SE1 9GF

WilliamCollinsBooks.com

First published in Great Britain in 2019 by William Collins

19 20 LSC/C 10 9 8 7 6 5 4 3 2

ISBN 978-0-00-831372-2

Typeset by Palimpsest Book Production Ltd, Falkirk, Stirlingshire

Printed and bound in the United States of America by LSC Communications

For more information visit: www.harpercollins.co.uk/green

Things really matter to me.
David Bowie, *Afraid*

CONTENTS

INTRODUCTION:
DAVID BOWIE - A LIFE STORY

'Dad lived ten lives in the years he had!' Duncan Jones's cheerful tweet on the second anniversary of his father's death, in January 2018, sums up the popular idea of David Bowie: a man who lived at an accelerated rate and transformed himself with the release of each new LP. In the 1970s alone, he raced from his folk-rock beginnings through Ziggy Stardust, Aladdin Sane, the Thin White Duke, and the blue-eyed soul man of *Young Americans*, before moving into the introspective Berlin period and finally concluding the decade on the cusp of the mainstream, MTV success that would dominate his 1980s.

It's a familiar story, retold in every biography. This introduction is not that story. This is the story of how my life intersected with David Bowie; how he informed and inspired me from my first encounter with my mum's *Let's Dance* cassette when I was thirteen. It is not about Bowie's changes, but about how he changed me – from that chance discovery in 1983 to 2015, when I undertook an academic project to live like him for a year, and attempted to compress his entire extraordinary career into twelve months.

Every Bowie fan has a story of the role he played in their life. Mine is unique, just like everyone else's. The purpose of this introduction is not to qualify me as an extraordinary super-fan – although my experience was certainly unusual – but as a fan like millions of others; as a fan, no doubt, like you. We all have our own sense of Bowie, and that is the point.

David Robert Jones was born on 8 January 1947 and died on 10 January 2016. David Bowie was born, as a stage name, on 16 September 1965. He never really died. 'David Bowie' was a persona created by Jones, but he thrived and survived for four decades not just because David Jones stuck with this name – he'd previously adopted 'Luther Jay', 'Alexis Jay' and 'Tom Jones' – but because his audiences embraced him: because of his fans.

Bowie became a star, a concept, a cultural icon, because of people like you and me, who took him wholeheartedly into their lives. We invested aspects of ourselves in him, and so a part of him continues in us. This book is a celebration of

Bowie's importance, and an exploration of his legacy as a cultural icon. But on another level, it's also about celebrating our inner Bowie, and letting it change and inspire us. We are 'all the millions here' Bowie gazed at in 'The Man Who Sold the World' in 1970: we are the galaxy of blackstars that he left behind in 2016. We all have our own stories of how he entered our lives and what he meant to us. This is mine.

I was born the year before Duncan Jones, and so while I knew of David Bowie in the 1970s, he stood for something shocking, scandalous and grown-up. He was like the taste of wine or beer: something I assumed I'd understand and appreciate later. When the video for 'Ashes to Ashes' played on *Top of the Pops* in 1980, I found it unpleasant and a bit scary, with its distorted colours, surreal images and flat, repetitive vocals. The droning chorus reminded me of the graffiti I saw on my walk home from school on the wall of a south London housing estate: 'Sex is good, sex is funky. Sex is best without a dunky.' Every week, I wanted the video to end so I could see more of ABBA, Blondie or Adam and the Ants.

But I changed, and Bowie changed. In 1983 I was on holiday with my family, somewhere in the English countryside: seven days of steam train museums, hill walks and horses. I picked up a cassette my mum had brought along: Bowie's *Let's Dance*, his mainstream breakthrough. My mum was thirty-eight at the time, only two years older than Bowie. I was thirteen. I slotted the tape into the red plastic Walkman I'd got for Christmas, and didn't take it out all week. My mum never got that cassette back. I still have it now. I asked her recently why she'd bought *Let's Dance*, as I didn't remember her being a Bowie fan in the seventies. She was 'entranced', she told me: he looked stunningly handsome and desirable, rather than just weird. She even tuned in to *Top of the Pops* every week, she confessed, to watch the videos. I felt exactly the same way, though we never told each other at the time.

For me in 1983, Bowie's music was a soundtrack to imaginary films, the music playing during the love scenes and end credits of movies that were never made. It was a glimpse into a sophisticated, adult world – not deliberately shocking, like his singles of the 1970s, but gleaming and stylish, with lyrical cross-references and casually dropped ideas that hinted at the intelligence behind them. *March of flowers!* he declared on the discordant 'Ricochet'. *March of dimes! These are the prisons! These are the crimes!* I listened repeatedly, carefully writing down the words; I felt like I was engaging with something challenging and avant-garde. I analysed them as if they were a poem from English class.

It wasn't easy to fit in at my school – you needed just the right Farah trousers and Pringle sweaters, the right sports bag, the right haircut and the right couldn't-care-less attitude. I studied too hard and couldn't afford all the proper gear, so I was a boffin, a tramp and probably a poof too. Lads at school said David Bowie was gay. I loved looking at his videos. I recorded them from the *Max Headroom* TV show, rewinding and freeze-framing them. I liked his sharp suits, his sharp teeth and his pained expression, as if he were struggling with something. In the 'Let's Dance' video, backed against the wall of an Australian bar and surrounded by the glares of hard-drinking men, he didn't look like he fitted in either.

Maybe I was gay for feeling that way about David Bowie, but he made me feel it didn't matter.

It turned out I wasn't gay, and it turned out Bowie wasn't either. It didn't matter. We both got married, to women. Nobody told me the groom wasn't meant to have his own theme song playing when he walks down the aisle, so I entered to an instrumental version of 'Modern Love', wearing a suit I thought Bowie would appreciate. I landed a job as a university lecturer. One winter, towards the end of the last century, I flew to Australia for a conference, via Japan. I took a new Walkman, with only one cassette: a personal Bowie collection I'd compiled for the trip. It was my first time alone on the other side of the world. I listened to nothing but Bowie for a week, discovering new songs as I walked by the Brisbane River under the surprising December sun. On the way back I was stuck at Narita Airport, and was taken by coach to a remote hotel overnight. I knew nobody, and didn't speak a word of the language. I'd never felt further from home. I listened to one song, on repeat. Now 'Ashes to Ashes' made sense to me, in all its alien strangeness and isolation.

I changed, and Bowie changed with me. I feel he was travelling alongside me, on that journey and on many others – or rather, that my own version of Bowie was my companion, because this 'Bowie' was a person I had helped to create, through our experiences together since 1983. You had your own version of him, no doubt – similar but different – who played a part in your life, and was shaped by the moments you shared.

Bowie and I both grew older. I was promoted to professor. Bowie seemed to enter semi-retirement, then returned ten years later with a comeback album in 2013. And that October, Lou Reed died. He was Bowie's old friend, of course, since the sixties — Bowie was one of the first British fans of the Velvet Underground — and I'd loved Lou's music since the eighties. But more importantly, I knew Lou Reed was only five years older than Bowie, and the refrain from the old song now sounded like a warning. *Five years, that's all we've got.* My rock idols were dying, already. I'd always assumed Bowie would go on for ever, and suddenly I came to terms with his mortality. He was in his mid-sixties now. I wanted to do something to thank him, to celebrate him, to pay tribute to him, while he was still alive.

Like every kid, I used to draw, and sing and dance. At nursery and infant school, we're encouraged to dress up, to perform and paint. We all do it, without shame and without a sense of being good or bad. And like most of us, I started to give those things up from adolescence onwards. It was hard enough as a teenager, trying to fit in, without having artistic hobbies too; and school also encouraged my generation to progressively narrow down, to focus only on what we were best at. Eight O-levels — my year was the first to introduce GCSEs — and three A-levels, then one subject at university, with a possible minor. (I rebelled in a small way by choosing a degree that was half English, half film: I even included an analysis of a Bowie video in a third-year essay.) By the time I was eighteen, I'd accepted that my drawing and singing were average at best, and that I was good at research and writing. So that's what I did as a career. I became an academic. And in 2013 I decided to study Bowie as an academic project. I began my research in May 2015.

I started by drawing up lists, from biographies and online sources, of all the books Bowie had read; then all the songs he'd listened to, and all the films he'd enjoyed. By immersing myself in his creative input – the art and culture that had influenced him – I hoped to gain a new understanding of his work. In Australia and Japan I'd listened to nothing but Bowie for a week. Now I was committing myself to his music for a year. I structured twelve months of my life around the various phases of his career, from the late 1960s to the present day, and devoted myself to one album at a time. As a sign of that commitment, I had my hair cut and coloured in the *Man Who Fell to Earth* style from the mid-1970s. I wanted to be reminded of my project every time I saw my own reflection. I wanted to connect with him, to merge with him in some way; to become an in-between Brooker-Bowie hybrid. As Bowie knew, '*Die Brücke*' is both the name of an art move-ment, and the German for 'bridge'. It's also, of course, a near-rhyme for my own name. It seemed to fit. I was trying to build a bridge between us.

Immersing myself in his influences wasn't enough. I grew up about six miles from David Jones, and I spent the summer of 2015 exploring his childhood and teenage territories, walking his old streets and discreetly checking out the houses where he'd lived with his family. I trained in filmmaking and photography in my twenties – again, something I gave up as a career – so I'd mixed with hair and make-up artists, but never had the experience of being on the other side of the camera, under the lights. I decided I needed to try it. I had photos taken of me, styled as Ziggy Stardust and Aladdin Sane. I posted them online. *Times Higher Education* magazine got in touch to find out what I was doing – a professor spending the summer break dressed as Bowie was enough for a news feature – and published a short article. Then other magazines got in touch, and newspapers, and radio, and then TV shows. I had progressed to the Thin White Duke phase – I'd commissioned a tailor for an authentically 1970s white shirt with a tall, wide collar – by the time *This Morning* asked me on for an interview with Eamonn Holmes. The next day, I got up early for a slot on Sky's news show, then took a taxi to a studio at midnight for a live broadcast in Australia. 'What are you doing next?' the reporters asked me. 'I'm going to Berlin,' I told them. And so I had to go to Berlin.

I was contacted by media and literary agents. I was invited to the Bowie exhibition as it toured to Melbourne, in Australia, and then to Groningen, in the Netherlands. I was interviewed in languages I didn't understand, and heard my words translated and voiced by an actor for news broadcasts around the world: I appeared in Swedish, Spanish, Russian and Portuguese newspapers. I'd become, in a small way, an international figure, borrowing something from Bowie's celebrity. I was performing different versions of myself, my personality splitting into public and private. I understood something of what Bowie must have experienced when he first became famous.

And then, in January 2016, Bowie died. I was in New York City that winter, wearing a replica I'd had made of his Alexander McQueen 'Earthling' coat; I'd had my hair clipped and spiked, and had grown a goatee beard, as he did for his fiftieth birthday. I was reliving Bowie's 1997 as I walked down another of his home streets – Lafayette, in Lower Manhattan – on a tour of his favourite bookstores and coffee shops. He was six storeys above me at the time, in his luxury apartment. He had a fortnight to live.

On 9 January I was back in Berlin, shooting footage for a video diary of my experiences. I'd been drawn into photography and film again; I'd also dug out my old cine camera and was using Super-8 for the first time since my teens. I flew home late that night. In the morning, the news felt like a bad dream. I did one interview, then refused the rest. I felt too shocked and sad, and had nothing much to say. That evening, I accepted an invitation from Radio 4, with director Julien Temple. We had a drink after the discussion, in a pub near the BBC with a dripping ceiling. He told me how Bowie had reacted to his half-brother's death in 1985. (I never met the real Bowie – only my own internal Bowie – but that year, I met a lot of people who'd known him personally.)

I experienced what felt like genuine grief, as if a family member had died. Many fans felt the same: maybe you did, too. I stayed indoors, and retreated inside myself. I'd been working with a tribute band, the Thin White Duke, taking the place of their lead singer, but it was months before I performed with them again – not until May, towards the end of my research year, and by that point it felt like time for a celebration rather than mourning. The gig was packed with long-term fans in their fifties, mixed with younger people of undergraduate age. When we sang 'Starman' as an encore, everyone joined in. I still have the footage, panning over the crowd of faces as they chant the final chorus. It's a picture of pure, shared joy. We were all thanking our own version of Bowie, and it felt like he was there with us.

As I approached May 2016, and the end of my project, I saw a counsellor for six sessions. I felt I needed a bridge of my own: a way to transition out of this intense research and back into everyday life. We started by talking about Bowie, and progressed to my own family, my personal history and what I'd inherited from previous generations, like my granddad in the Navy, who never talked about what he'd seen in conflict. Bowie, born just after the war, and growing up around Brixton bombsites, was about expression, creativity and release, an antidote to English repression. He was about the bravery not to care if you fitted in with the norm, about the boldness to push past your own limits. He wasn't the best singer – Freddie Mercury soars above him on 'Under Pressure' – and he certainly wasn't the best dancer. He tended to play himself, as an actor, and he was only ever an amateur painter. But he did it anyway. And, because I had to, because I'd committed to my research project, I did things I wasn't the best at, too.

As well as taking up film and photography again, using various formats from digital to 1960s vintage kit, I experimented with painting, because Bowie did it during his Berlin period. I was surprised by how much I enjoyed it. I wasn't very good at first, but I got better. I started going to portrait classes every week, and continued to improve. I began singing lessons, too, and while I'll never be the best, after four years of vocal training I'm not so bad. I have folders on my computer now titled 'painting' and 'singing', where I save my own work and track its progress. I have Bowie to thank for that. I didn't become Bowie – nobody can – but by aspiring to be more like him, I became a better, brighter, bolder version of myself.

I am a Bowie fan, but I am also a professor, and those two sides of me are bridged rather than separate. I've published scholarly articles and an academic book about Bowie, which were informed by both critical theory and my decades of fandom; and I became more deeply invested in

Bowie through my writing and research, as I learned more about him and studied his work more closely. I even taught a class on Bowie and stardom, enjoying the way twenty-one-year-old students, who were born around Bowie's fiftieth birthday and the *Earthling* album, both appreciated and criticised his star persona.

Those twin approaches – fan and academic – come together in this book. For me, critical theory and philosophy are only useful if they serve us as tools; if they offer us a new under-standing and a valuable perspective. So the use of theorists like Fredric Jameson, Mikhail Bakhtin, Jacques Derrida, Gilles Deleuze and Félix Guattari in this book is not to try to elevate Bowie's popular work to some loftier academic plane – to show that he is worthy of serious analysis and that his name can be mentioned with theirs. That, to me, goes without saying. Their theories are here as tools to give us a different angle and context for Bowie's creative expressions, identity transitions and cultural references. They can offer us a new way of seeing, which is surely what Bowie was all about.

If you love David Bowie, you already know why he matters. You have your own reasons, bound up with moments from your own life when his songs intersected with your experiences and provided the perfect soundtrack. But this book will suggest different reasons, approaching from new directions and new angles: new ways of connecting the dots and mapping a path through the mosaic of his life.

1

BECOMING

On 25 March 2018, a statue of Bowie – or rather, of several Bowies, because it morphed multiple incarnations into a bronze chimera – was unveiled in the market square of Aylesbury. Its title is *Earthly Messenger*. The aesthetic was criticised, but the name passed without comment, because it perfectly fits the new persona that has evolved posthumously around David Bowie: the idea of an otherworldly being who descended to our planet in January 1947 and departed it in January 2016.

'Ziggy is Stardust now', was the caption on one memorial cartoon, showing Aladdin Sane's face as a new constellation: and indeed, the 'Stardust for Bowie' campaign named a lightning-bolt pattern of stars in the vicinity of Mars after him. Others evoked Major Tom: an astronaut stepping through the Pearly Gates, or a weeping Ground Control sending unanswered messages to the lost spaceman. One artist drew Bowie in delicate watercolours, in the style of the Little Prince: Ziggy standing on his own tiny planet in space, titled *The Man Who Fell to Earth*.

Time, in turn, published a commemorative edition called 'His Time on Earth'. Blogs, articles and tweets repeated the phrase 'Goodbye, Starman', elaborating on the theme with each anniversary: 'A year ago, the Starman David Bowie said goodbye to our planet to start his "Space Oddity",' an online fan noted in January 2017, while *Vice* marked 'a year since David Bowie ascended'. 'It's been two years since David Bowie left us for his home planet, and we haven't been the same since,' suggested the *Consequences of Sound* site in January 2018, under the headline 'Remembering the Man Who Fell to Earth, Two Years After Bowie Returned to the Stars'.

Of course, Bowie provided the raw material for this final media incarnation, which joins the dots of various songs and characters – Starman, Lady Stardust, Blackstar, Major Tom, the Man Who Fell to Earth and, more fundamentally, the idea of Ziggy as messiah – into the picture of an uncanny visitor from outer space, an 'Earthly Messenger', whether alien or angel. Fans can hardly be blamed for extending Bowie's career-long fascination with outer space into a comforting image – somewhere between religion and science fiction – of him not dead, but departed to another world; he even advised them on his final album to 'look up here, I'm in heaven'. But even at the time, this idea felt to me like a misreading, understandable as a coping mechanism but disrespectful to his mourning family – Duncan Jones, I guessed, did not think of his father as an extraterrestrial who'd returned to his home planet – and misrepresentative of the Bowie I felt I knew.

My own sense of Bowie was not of an uncanny creature who had descended, fully-formed, to treat us to his art before leaving us again. I saw 'Bowie' as a persona originally conceived by the young David Jones, who struggled for success and worked hard to maintain and develop it. Part of the point of Bowie, to me, is that Jones was, contrary to the popular myth, an ambitious, frustrated and creative young man from an ordinary environment, who created something extraordinary through sustained effort, dedication and drive in the face of repeated failure. To see him as a creature who effortlessly came and went from the stars diminishes that other side of the story: to my mind, this more complex version is the truer story, though, as we'll see, the truth of Bowie is elusive.

The Aylesbury statue points to another, contradictory way of seeing Bowie that emerged after his death. He was supposedly from elsewhere, but he was also from, or associated with, specific places on earth, and those places wanted to claim him for tourism. Aylesbury's boast was that the *Ziggy Stardust* album had debuted there – though Ziggy himself first performed at the Toby Jug in Tolworth, down the road from me – and argued that its Market Square, the site of the statue, inspired the first line of 'Five Years'. South-east London maintained that Bowie was 'Our Brixton Boy' – the slogan appeared on the Ritzy Cinema just after his death – and has its own mural, now repainted and protected with a plastic cover, around the corner from his childhood home on Stansfield Road.

Strictly speaking, yes, he was a Brixton boy; he was born on that street, at number 40. But his family moved when he was barely six, and he lived in Bromley from January 1953 onwards, including a full ten years in the same house on Plaistow Grove. Brixton in south London sounds better as an origin than Bromley in Kent, as Bowie surely realised when he dropped tall tales about getting into local 'street brawls' that made him 'very butch' and growing up in an ''ouseful of blacks'. Brixton, in the early 1950s, was a borderline between the past and the future, where bombsites and ration books were reminders of the recent war, but where the sights and tastes of a more multicultural, modern London had begun to creep in. One neighbour recalls technicolour clothing, Caribbean vegetables, even jugglers and sword-swallowers at the local market, while Bowie describes the streets around Stansfield Road as 'like Harlem'. Bromley, on the other hand, apart from its associations with H. G. Wells, is known primarily for bland suburbia: biographer Christopher Sandford mentions it as a 'drab, featureless dormitory town', and Bowie referred scathingly, in a 1993 interview, to its regularity, its conformity and its 'meanness'. For much of his life, he preferred to write it out of his official history.

But think about your own childhood: where you were born, and where you actually grew up. I was born in Coventry and spent my earliest years there in a council flat, but by the time I turned three my parents had moved to the first of many short-term lets in south-east London. I only half remember those from photographs, unsure if my memory is of the image or the real place; and I don't recall Coventry at all. Certainly, I was born there, but the streets I'm from – the streets that really formed me – are the ones around Kinveachy Gardens in Charlton from ages three to eleven, and then Woodhill, down the hill in neighbouring Woolwich, as a teenager.

Did his first six years in Brixton shape David Jones? To some extent, no doubt. 'I left Brixton when I was still quite young, but that was enough to be very affected by it,' he later claimed. 'It left strong images in my mind.' He apparently returned to Stansfield Road in 1991, asking the tour bus to stop outside his old house, and came back for a final pilgrimage with his daughter in 2014. But Brixton's influence must surely pale compared to the formative decade, from ages seven to seventeen, that David Jones spent at 4 Plaistow Grove, next to Sundridge Park Station, in Bromley. There is, as yet, no statue, plaque, or mural there – just occasional flowers outside someone else's residential house – though he recalled it in 1993's 'Buddha of Suburbia', with one of those lyrics that seems a gift to biographers: 'Living in lies by the railway line, pushing the hair from my eyes. Elvis is English and climbs the hills . . . can't tell the bullshit from the lies.' 'I knew him as Bromley Dave,' Bowie's childhood friend Paul Reeves confirmed, years later. 'As that is where we were both from.'

When I attempted to immerse myself in Bowie's life and career, between 2015 and 2016, I followed the path he'd traced around the world, from New York to Berlin to Switzerland to New York again. I also spent time at his old haunts in London, reading his recollections of the La Gioconda coffee shop at 9 Denmark Street while sitting in the same spot, currently a Flat Iron steak restaurant. But while I'd visited his home streets in Bromley – Canon Road, Clarence Road and Plaistow Grove – I'd only paid passing attention to the area. With hindsight, there was an unconscious reason behind the omission.

My old manor, around Kinveachy Gardens and Woodhill, is about six miles from Bowie's house in Bromley; close enough that we both knew each other's territory, growing up. He travelled to Woolwich at least once, to see Little Richard at the Granada. My experience and his also overlapped in Blackheath and Lewisham, equidistant between our childhood homes: we both visited friends in the posh big houses of

Blackheath and travelled to Lewisham for its superior shops. There are key differences, of course, and I'm flattering myself by imagining a connection between us. When Bowie caught the bus to Lewisham to buy shoes and shirts, he jumped off it two stops later with 'Life on Mars?' already in his head. In significant ways, then, my experience in Woolwich was not like David Bowie's in Bromley: but there are interesting cultural continuities, despite our difference in age. Our town centres had a lot in common, for instance: a Littlewoods with its school uniforms and jam doughnuts; the knives, forks and tomato-shaped ketchup dispensers in Wimpy's very English hamburger restaurants; ornate, art deco Odeon cinemas on the edge of town. Because Bromley already seemed familiar to me from my own childhood, I didn't delve as deeply in, or investigate it, in such detail. So in May 2018, I reopened the investigation. I went to live in Bromley, to revisit Bowie's time there. I ate there, drank there, slept there and shopped there, walking his old routes.

To me, research – and critical thinking in general – is not so much about finding information as it is about making connections: drawing lines, linking points and sometimes making unexpected leaps across time and space. If you plotted them visually, the paths of my research process would form a network, a matrix: a conceptual map, expanding and developing and becoming increasingly more complex.

I started with a map: with two maps. The Goad Plan, a

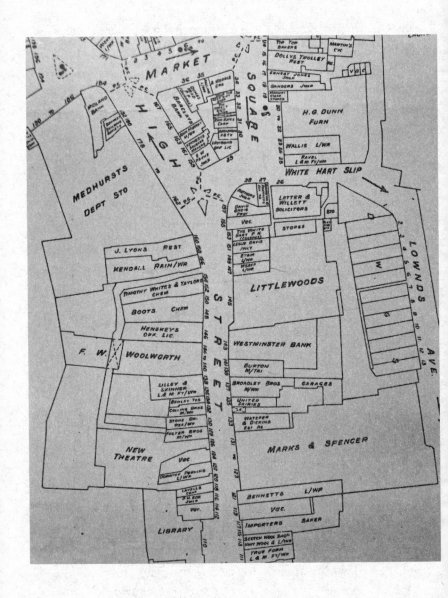

gigantic, hand-drawn map of Bromley in the 1960s, spread across a table in the library's Historic Collections room, and a far smaller, digital version alongside it on my phone – 2018's Google Maps app – which I scrolled across for comparison. The same place, separated in time.

There is little sign now of the smaller boutiques and quirky, independent shops that would have been part of David Jones's cultural landscape – the Tip Top Bakery, Sherry's Fabrics, Terry's Stores, Dolly's Trolley – though there is a Tips and Toes nail salon, and Buddy's Café. Some of Bromley's newer shops and venues offer an ersatz simulation of the past. Mr Simm's Olde Sweet Shop is a franchise dating back to 2004, and Greater than Gatsby, a bar promising 1920s style, warns its punters: 'Guys, no hats or hoodies, come on, you're not 12.'

Medhurst's Department Store, where Bowie bought his American vinyl and listened to records in the basement sound booths, is now a Primark. Wimpy's, where he ate burgers with his school-friend Geoff MacCormack, indulging his tastes for America, is the Diner's Inn Café. The nearby Lyons' Corner House, where teenagers could gather over coffee, has also vanished – it's now a Mothercare – though there's still a music store, Reid's, with saxophones in the window.

I sat at the Stonehenge Café, opposite Primark, and watched the Market Square and High Street with a double vision. It wasn't hard to imagine a teenage David walking through the doors – past where the Aladdin Sane T-shirts are now hanging – to meet his girlfriend Jane Green, who worked on the record counter, for a covert smooch to Eddie Cochran and Ray Charles. 'Can't Help Thinking About Me', says one of Bowie's 1960s singles. I couldn't help thinking about him. One of his last songs – released posthumously, on 8 January 2017 – was called 'No Plan'. His final tracks in particular feel like a puzzle he left behind, a message for his followers. What was his plan, during the 1960s? Did he have any sense of his end goal? Was he working his way towards fame, or just enjoying the scene, the lifestyle, the groups and the girls, like so many other teenage boys who loved records and made their own music?

Pulling the digital map back from the High Street to a wider view, we can begin to plot Bowie's Bromley on a broader scale. Most of the key landmarks in his early life are all within walking distance of each other; I proved it to myself by walking between them, putting the legwork into my research. Only Bowie's secondary school, Bromley Tech, was out of easy reach; he used to take the number 410 bus. It's now Ravens Wood School, and I visited it for the final chapter of this book.

Plaistow Grove is less than a mile north of the town centre. I took a right at the Hop and Rye pub, then walked down College Lane, passing St Mary's Church, where a seven-year-old Bowie sang in the choir with his friends George

Underwood and Geoff MacCormack. Nearby is a chip shop that dates back to 1920: I wondered if the lads got a take-away there, as I did. Their Cub Scout pack, the 18th Bromley, is still based at the church, and meets every Friday. Past Plaistow Green, a well-tended grassy square, it's another fifteen minutes down quiet, safe streets to David's former primary school, Burnt Ash.

The Bromel Club, in the Bromley Court Hotel, is another mile from Plaistow Grove, along London Lane. Bowie played there with the Lower Third in 1966, aged nineteen: it was a prestigious gig, in a venue that also hosted the Yardbirds, the Kinks and Jimi Hendrix. The exterior has barely changed, but the Jazz Club became a ballroom, which became the Garden Restaurant, a gorgeous space of curved archways and elegant pillars. There are photos of Bowie with a mod haircut on display in the hotel reception, with a mounted single of his early songs with the Lower Third and The Manish Boys.

Sitting in the restaurant, I studied a different kind of matrix: a list of names and numbers, from an old reference book called *Kelly's Directory*. It told me exactly who had lived on Bowie's street and in the surrounding area in specific years. Even the abbreviations carried an air of quaint, pre-war convention. Every George was shortened to Geo., every William was a Wm. There were Herberts, Cuthberts, Cyrils and Arthurs; the Misses Austin, Miss Osborn and Miss Gibbs.

I spoke to residents who'd lived on Plaistow Grove at the same time as Bowie. Some of them remembered him, or had stories about him passed down from previous generations. One told me that her nan saw David with his mother regularly at Mr Bull's greengrocer shop. 'She always tied coloured ribbons in his hair as a toddler because she wanted a girl. No wonder he turned out weird!' Bromley's older locals confirmed the shops around the corner from the Jones family, all the owners known politely by their surname. Mr and Mrs Bull had a dog called Curry. The Kiosk, selling sweets at Sundridge Park Station, was run by Miss Violet Hood; then there was Coates electrical engineers, Arthur Ash boot repair, Bailey's the newsagent, a butcher's shop run by two brothers, and a hair salon variously known at different times as Beryl's or Paul's.

Plaistow Lane, the main road, slopes slightly uphill before the turn on to Bowie's home street. A painted sign brands the area as Sundridge Village. On a sunny evening in spring, it looks like a great place to grow up. David Jones's neighbours did not change at all between 1955, when he was eight, and 1967, when he turned twenty. There was Miss Florence West, to the left at number 2, and to the right, Mr Harry Hall; Mr George Rowe lived at number 8, and Mr and Mrs Pollard at number 10. None of them moved in or out during those twelve years. On that specific, local level, Bowie's life on Plaistow Grove seems consistent to the point of being comatose.

Walking down the short, quiet street from the main road to his house – morning, Miss West, good morning, Mr Hall – you can easily imagine an ambitious, imaginative and creative teenager becoming bored. From his back bedroom he could hear the trains from Sundridge Park on their way to London, and the music and boozy crowds from the pub, the Crown Hotel, at the end of his garden. I talked to a resident who'd occupied the same room, after the Jones family left. She explained that you couldn't hear the trains anymore, now that the windows were double-glazed. Times change. The Crown is now Cinnamon Culture, an upmarket Indian. I sat in the beer garden. You can see what would have been his bedroom window, from the back, and imagine him again, looking out at the lights, the trains, the adults in couples and groups; listening to the music from the pub as it mixed with his American radio broadcasts, and longing for escape.

Of course, it's only imagination. We can establish certain facts, but then we choose how to fill in the gaps. Without Bowie's long-promised but never-written autobiography, we can only rely on available documentary evidence like maps and directories, and the recollections of his friends, family members and acquaintances, decades later. But judging by the jokes, provocations and outright lies that constitute many of Bowie's interviews, can we really assume that even his own memoirs would be any more reliable?

Every biography of Bowie, even the most authoritative, is

a constellation created by joining together a scatter of stars into a convincing picture. It is a particular route, plotted across the points of a map, which leaves some paths untravelled. It is a selection of ideas and evidence from the Bowie matrix – the vast network of what we know about this public figure and private man – which emphasises some details, and discards others. That's the nature of research and writing: not just the discovery of information but the way we join it up; what we omit, as well as what we include. A history of Bowie – like any other history – is a story, based around selection, interpretation, speculation and deletion. It has to be, because if biographers simply absorbed and channelled all the available information about Bowie's life, it would overwhelm any sense of conventional narrative and character: put simply, it wouldn't even make sense.

In 1967, for instance, Bowie told a *New Musical Express* journalist that he'd moved with his family not to Bromley, but to Yorkshire when he was eight. He claimed to have lived with an uncle in an ancient farmhouse, 'surrounded by open fields and sheep and cattle', complete with a seventeenth-century monk's hole where Catholic priests had hidden from Protestant persecution. The *NME* journalist commented helpfully that it was 'a romantic place for a child to grow'. There's a seed of truth in what sounds a purely fanciful story: Kevin Cann's *Any Day Now: The London Years*, built around well-documented details, suggests that David did visit his Uncle

Jimmy in Yorkshire for holidays in 1952 and fabricated these trips into an extended stay at a later age. Yet even this contradicts Bowie's simultaneous assertion that he lived in Brixton until the age of ten or eleven and walked to school past the gates of its prison. Authors Peter and Leni Gillman dug into educational archives to confirm that David Jones transferred into Burnt Ash Juniors, Bromley, on 20 June 1955. The school is seven miles from Brixton Prison, which makes it very unlikely that a ten-year-old took that detour. Historical records and maps, with their prosaic evidence, are duller than Bowie's stories about his past, but more reliable.

Can we trust the memories of the people who grew up with him? Dana Gillespie, one of Bowie's first girlfriends, memorably describes a trip to his parents' 'tiny little working-class house . . . the smallest I'd ever been in'. She thinks they had 'little tuna sandwiches . . . it was a really cold house, a very chilly atmosphere.' There was a television 'blasting away in the corner, and nobody spoke'. She repeated the anecdote for Francis Whately's 2019 documentary, *David Bowie: Finding Fame*, adding a postscript: 'It was hard going. It was soulless.'

David Jones's mother Margaret, known as Peggy, is similarly described by his former school-friends as cold and unaffectionate: 'I don't think it was a family,' remembered Dudley Chapman. 'It was a lot of people who happened to be living under the same roof.' George Underwood agrees: 'Even David didn't like his mum. She wasn't an easy person to get on with.' Geoff MacCormack remembers telling Bowie that Peggy 'never quite took to me', receiving the rueful confession in response that 'she never quite took to me, either.' Peter Frampton suggests that David had a better relationship with his teacher, Owen Frampton – Peter's dad – than he did with his own father, Hayward Stenton (known as 'John') Jones. 'I'm not privy to the relationship . . . but I don't think it was that great.'

George Underwood, by contrast, recalls John Jones as 'lovely, a really nice gentle man', while Bowie's cousin, Kristina Amadeus, points out that David's dad, who 'absolutely doted on him', bought him a plastic saxophone, a tin guitar and a xylophone before he was an adolescent, and that 'he also owned a record player when few children had one . . . David's father took him to meet singers and other performers preparing for the Royal Variety Performance.' The Jones's house may have seemed tiny to Dana Gillespie, but to Kristina, it was 'lower middle class . . . his father was from a very affluent family.' Uncle John, she tells the Gillmans, 'really wanted him to be a star'. Note that despite these many documented friendships and relationships with cousins close to his age, Bowie reports of his childhood that 'I was lonely,' and also recalled: 'I was a kid that loved being in my room reading books and entertaining ideas. I lived a lot in my imagination. It was a real effort to become a social animal.'

Despite the supposed coldness of the Jones family home,

Bowie reminisced in the late 1990s about roast dinners on wintry Sundays, with a small fire blazing, and his mother's voice soaring to match the songs on the radio. 'Oh, I love this one,' she'd remark, joining in with 'O For the Wings of a Dove', before haranguing John Jones for thwarting her musical ambitions. David Buckley's biography describes her as a 'drama queen' with a frustrated dream of 'being a singer, being a star', while John was 'naturally nonconfrontational'. Frigid, unaffectionate, not really a family; or a warm, even heated environment, with a drama-queen mother and a softly-spoken dad who used his industry connections, his experience as head of Dr Barnardo's publicity department, and his comfortably middle-class salary to support his son's ambitions?

Bowie's former manager Kenneth Pitt, meanwhile, gives an impression of 4 Plaistow Grove that contrasts with Dana Gillespie's chilly image; and his version of Peggy is also far more doting. 'It was a very conventional suburban home, a tiny terraced house, very comfortable and very homely . . . and there I'd sit in the front room, talking about David, and his mother would tell me, "You know, he was always the prettiest boy in the street, the sort of boy that all the neighbours loved."'

Biographer Christopher Sandford adds to the complexity of this family portrait. David's father was 'irrepressibly proud of his son' but also 'dour, taciturn and tight-fisted – a cold man, an unresponsive man' who had a stream of affairs and was 'very prejudiced . . . very'. Peggy, by contrast, was 'loud, fractious and given to bewildering mood swings', yet also 'inhibiting and aloof'. Sandford finds quotes from Bowie to support this perspective: his father 'had a lot of love in him, but he couldn't express it. I can't remember him ever touching me', while a compliment from his mother 'was very hard to come by. I would get my paints out and all she could say was, "I hope you're not going to make a mess."'

Peggy herself told an origin myth of Bowie. When he was three, she explained to a journalist in 1985, he'd taken an 'unnatural' interest in the contents of her make-up bag. 'When I found him, he looked for all the world like a clown. I told him that he shouldn't use make-up, but he said, "You do, Mummy."' It's a neat story, and it echoes her son's memory of being scolded for playing with paints, as well as his later glam, drag and Pierrot personae. But with hindsight, knowing what David Jones became, it's understandable if those who knew him, even his mother, tend to tell stories that fit the finished picture, and if biographers, in turn, choose those as the building-blocks of their books. Our sense of David Jones's childhood is a mixture of non-fiction, invention and half-truth, shaped retro-actively by everyone's awareness of what happened next. The adult Bowie – sometimes literally – rewrites the past of young Jones, and those who knew him tend to follow suit.

Underwood, for instance, remembers that David boasted precociously to the school careers adviser, 'I want to be a saxophonist in a modern jazz quartet.' Owen Frampton recalls the Bowie of Bromley Tech as 'quite unpredictable . . . already a cult figure'. Dana Gillespie claims Bowie told her, at age fourteen, 'I want to get out of here. I have to get out of here. I want to go up in the world.' A neighbour tells Sandford that Bowie used to stand in the glow of the Crown pub's coaching-lantern, 'anticipating his pose as Ziggy Stardust'. Another relative recalls that he stood up in front of the TV, aged nine, and announced, 'I can play guitar just like the Shads . . . and he did' – even though the Shadows didn't appear in public until David was eleven. The local anecdote about Peggy taking her infant son to the shops with ribbons in his hair – 'No wonder he turned out weird!' – falls into the same pattern. Even the midwife who delivered baby David in 1947 supposedly pronounced, eerily prefiguring the image of Bowie as angel messiah, that 'this child has been on earth before'. His music teacher, Mrs Baldry, is unusual in her careful refusal to fuel the Bowie myth. 'He was no spectacular singer. You'd never have picked him out and said, "That boy sings wonderfully."' Bowie's own revisions of his past, of course, don't help. 'I've always been camp since I was seven,' he claimed. 'I was outrageous then.' His tendency to retcon his own origins – to suggest that the seeds of his later strangeness and stardom were already rooted in childhood – is particularly evident in his 1970s interviews, when he was keenly forging his media brand.

'Can't tell the bullshit from the lies.' As ever, Bowie's lyric was knowing. The truth, inevitably, lies in an amalgam of all these testimonies – the interviews, the reminiscences, the dry documents – with the likeliest possibilities emerging in the overlaps between stories, or in a combination of apparently contradictory reports. A house can be tiny, poky and cold to one visitor; tiny, cosy and warm to another. A man can find it difficult to express physical affection towards his son, but show his love by buying him instruments and introducing him to celebrities. A mother can praise her boy as the prettiest in the street, but still feel wary of him playing with her make-up. A woman can sing without shame to the radio over a family Sunday dinner, and still seem aloof or uncomfortable in front of a fourteen-year-old girlfriend. A teenager can have many friends and still feel lonely.

The information we have about Bowie in Bromley (and in London, and Berlin, and New York) is a complex mosaic: Dylan Jones's *David Bowie: A Life*, a collection of short inter-views from which some of the quotations above are taken, is a perfect example of a book's form echoing its subject. Bowie is, essentially, a kaleidoscope of multicoloured fragments, constantly shifting. We can identify patterns from the shapes, but someone else can look again from a different angle, and twist a little, and see something new. Our knowledge of him is a complex network, where two conflicting ideas can both have been true at once. 'Some writers have struggled to put all this in a logical sequence,' he told journalist George Tremlett in the late 1960s. 'I wouldn't bother if I were you.'

Why does this matter? It matters to remember that David Bowie did not descend to earth in 1947 but spent the longest stretch of his younger years in that tiny home on Plaistow Grove and in the streets surrounding it. He wasn't hanging out with glam rockers and groupies, but with Peggy and John Jones, with George and Geoff and Peter, and sometimes Kristina, and sometimes his half-brother Terry Burns. Ten years before Ziggy, he was the fourteen-year-old in his school photo, with a winning, wonky grin, a neat haircut and two perfectly normal eyes.

He was, in many ways, like the hundreds of other boys at Burnt Ash and Bromley Tech. He was also far from the only local lad to form a band as a teenager: his first group, The Konrads, was already well-established, with George Underwood as the vocalist, by the time David was allowed to join in June 1962. David Jones had talent and ambition, but so did a lot of young men in his social circle. Somehow, he made himself exceptional. Somehow, he emerged from this environment and created an act – a work of art – that the world had never seen before. The story matters because anyone could have done it, but only Bowie did: and the fact that a boy who grew up in Bromley could forge the persona of a world-conquering glam rock messiah is surely more inspiring to the rest of us than the idea that Bowie simply arrived from space, fully-formed.

So how did he do it? This is my own interpretation: my way of connecting points in the Bowie matrix to create a story.

The suburbs played a part. Novelist Jonathan Coe has written of his upbringing on the outskirts of Birmingham that 'it gave me the imaginative space to dream of different worlds; wider, more exciting, not necessarily better. It was the very uneventfulness of the suburbs that turned so many of us into creators.' Rupa Huq, in *Making Sense of Suburbia Through Popular Culture*, identifies locations like Bromley as a nowhere-land, neither 'city' nor 'country'. 'There is a case to be made,' she goes on, 'for the very fact that suburbs are seen as unremarkable and conformist allowing artistic endeavour to flourish there.' David Buckley agrees that 'the geography of the situation is crucial: living in the suburbs so close to London provided the perfect paradigm for escape. London represented exotica, freedom and change for youngsters driven to near-desperation by the blandness of the capital's environs. And it was close by – a mere half an hour away by train.' No wonder Bowie's back bedroom, where he listened to the radio within earshot of the railway line, looking out at the carriage lamp of a busy pub, is such a potent image in his origin myth.

Academics like the word 'liminal' for these spaces that lie in between, neither one thing nor the other; 'liminal' comes from the Latin for 'threshold'. David was outside, waiting and wanting to cross over.

'You find yourself in the middle of two worlds,' he reflected. 'There's the extreme values of people who grow up in the countryside, and the very urban feel of the city. In suburbia, you're given the impression that nothing, culturally, belongs to you. That you are, sort of, in this wasteland.' He dreamed not just of London but also beyond it, through the jazz records and Beat poetry Terry Burns brought back from Soho, to America. Young David, born exactly twelve years after Elvis, was already fired up on 'Hound Dog' and Little Richard's 'Tutti Frutti', and listened to the American Armed Forces Radio; by age thirteen he'd written to the US Navy via the embassy in London, and been invited to spend the day with them learning about American football. 'Then, much to his amazement,' the *Bromley and Kentish Times* reported in November 1960, 'David was presented with a helmet, set of shoulder pads and a football, all of which had been donated by a local Air Force base.' The news story features a photo of him in full football gear, and the headline 'David Leads Sport Revolution'.

We get a sense of the initiative, the ambition, the almost naïve confidence – if you don't ask, you don't get – that we associate with the later David Bowie, who drawled like a gangster in 'Sweet Thing/Candidate', from 1974: 'if you want it, boys, get it here.' But behind this remarkably enterprising teenager, a man stands in the wings: a secondary supporting character, reminding us that David's supposedly dull suburban life had other dimensions.

'It all started,' the local paper explains, 'when David's father, Mr Haywood Jones, purchased a short-wave radio with evenings of musical relaxation in mind for the family.' John Jones is also there in the background of his son's news stunt: 'His father, who comes from a family of avid rugby enthusiasts, stood by scratching his head, perplexed.' He takes the role of the boring suburbanite – 'it is a safe bet that the people of Bromley may soon be scratching their heads, too' – but it was John who escorted David (with George Underwood, who appears in some of the photos) up to Grosvenor Square for the day, and who bought the radio set in the first place. Jones Senior had already provided the house with a TV, in time for the coronation in 1953, and a stack of new American 45s, including David's beloved 'Tutti Frutti', in 1956. Bowie later enthused that when he first played Little Richard, 'My heart nearly burst with excitement. I'd never heard anything even resembling this. It filled the room with energy and colour and outrageous defiance. I had heard God. Now I wanted to see him.' If this is another convincing origin story for Bowie's stardom, his dad was behind it, quietly enabling his son's transformative experience.

David may have dreamed of escape from Bromley, but there are far worse things to escape than boredom. He had the leisure to experiment and play – to join bands, to try different fashions – because, despite the modest size of his house, he was cushioned by a comfortable level of middle-class privilege. In the year they moved to Plaistow Grove, David met new friends at the choir and the Cub Scouts, and was taken by his dad, with his cousin Kristina, to see Tommy Steele, getting his autograph backstage. His headmaster at Burnt Ash encouraged the class to express themselves through 'movement training', describing David as a 'sensitive and imaginative boy'. There were regular trips to his dad's work, more meetings with TV stars, and a Scout summer camp on the Isle of Wight, where George and David performed their favourite pop songs as a skiffle group.

John Jones took David to visit potential secondary schools; David got his first choice, Bromley Tech, 'with no real battle'. His form master, Owen Frampton, was progressive and inspirational, starting an 'art stream for students interested in visual creativity'. David decided he wanted to become a jazz musician, after reading *On the Road* in 1961: his dad bought him an acrylic sax for Christmas that year. Within a couple of weeks, David had persuaded his dad to help him buy a better one, and they went to Tottenham Court Road together to get a professional instrument on hire purchase. David set himself to the task of learning music from his American singles; self-disciplined for a fifteen-year-old, but no doubt helped by the fact that his house already had an upright piano. With his characteristic, wide-eyed chutzpah (if you want it, boys, get it here), David wrote to a local jazz musician, Ronnie Ross, asking for lessons. His proficiency on the sax got him into his first band, The Konrads, and his first public gig at a school fête. There was a network of local venues ready to accommodate them: church halls for rehearsals, country clubs, colleges and ballrooms. John Jones arranged the band's professional photoshoot. Although David left school with a single pass, his form master Owen Frampton made the effort to find him a job in advertising, which David was fired from a year later. 'I just couldn't stand the pace . . . it was just so boring trying to compete with sketching out raincoats and things.' His dad supported him financially as David decided to dedicate himself solely to making it in the music business. Both his parents signed his first management deal, because David was only seventeen. This was summer 1964, and he was in his third band already, having made his television debut in June.

We're getting ahead of ourselves: but as we piece together the story of how David Jones became Bowie, and how Bowie became Ziggy, it's important to remember that his background helped him – not just by giving him something to transcend and escape, but in a more literal sense. He faced obstacles and hardships, there's little doubt of that. The eye injury that

left him with a permanently-dilated left pupil sent him to
hospital – his dad rushed him in when it 'just exploded' – and
needed months of convalescence. He argued with his mother
in particular, who, concerned about his obsession with music
and fashion over schoolwork, 'wanted me turned down'. He
often had to retreat to his bedroom, thinking, in his own
words, 'they are not going to beat me.' (But didn't we all,
as teenagers?) And then there was Terry, and the family history
that Terry carried with him, which we'll come to later. But
he also had a father, at least, who ferried him around, funded
him and gave him many of the tools that forged his later,
larger-than-life persona. It was his dad, ironically – or with
self-sacrificing generosity – who helped his son to become
bigger and bolder than David Jones, to rewrite his childhood
and to ditch the family name.

But there were a lot of boys in bands in 1960s Bromley,
sharing similar levels of middle-class privilege, home comforts
and family support. David Jones's success was not, of course,
solely due to his dad. In the story so far, we can already sense
an incredible self-belief; for a supposedly sensitive, insular
teenager, he went straight for what he wanted. His music
career in the 1960s suggests a slow, steady attempt to
construct something original and distinctive from available
materials: a piecing-together of genres and styles, a testing
of what worked and a willingness to quickly reject what
didn't, and a struggle within the system to create something

new. He didn't want to be a great bluesman, a pop singer or a folk artist. He combined his talent for music with his flair for fashion and visual art, using them all as a means to an end. What he wanted was a certain type of stardom.

Shortly before joining The Konrads, he'd been inspired – on another theatre visit, to see *Stop the World, I Want to Get Off*, in July 1961 – by Anthony Newley's theatrical flair and his power over a crowd.

He kept saying 'Stop the world', and the cast would freeze, and he'd come forward and rap to the audience. Then he'd say 'OK' and they'd start moving again. The girls were like machines, lifting their arms and legs up and down like clock-work. It just blew me over and I knew I wanted some of that, but I didn't know what exactly. That's when I started formulating my own style.

Even if we take Bowie's tendency to retcon his past into account, we can trace this impulse through his early experiences with local bands. His dedication to the saxophone, thanks to Ronnie Ross, won him a place in The Konrads. He started to take on vocal duties and wrote some of his own songs, slipping them in between, as he said, the usual covers 'of anything that was in the charts'. They worked hard; they were a journeyman band, aiming to please the crowds of the Royal Bell in Bromley (now a boarded-up nightclub) and the

Beckenham Ballroom with versions of the Shadows and 'Johnny B. Goode'. Audiences stopped dancing and drifted away from the stage when the band switched to one of David's compositions, but he kept pushing, expanding them beyond a straightforward covers outfit. He challenged his own insecurities by singing two songs at each gig – 'I was never very confident of my voice' – and, perhaps to counter the shyness, started to invent a rock 'n' roll persona for himself. He told the others that Jones was a boring name, and toyed with Luther Jay and Alexis Jay before settling on Dave Jay, signing it with a saxophone on the capital letter.

The band's uniform of green corduroy jackets and brown mohair trousers was his idea too – as were the publicity pics with his dad's photographer friend – and he drew towering cartoon backdrops of jazz musicians for their later gigs, creating a distinctive sense of theatrical space.

A news report in the *Bromley and Kentish Times* of August 1963 explains that 'a feature of their stage act is the special infra-blue lights which, when directed on their specially coated instruments, cause them to change colour – a big hit with the fans.' The article doesn't specify that it was David's idea, but we can take a guess. Earlier in 1963 he'd failed to persuade the other boys to rename the band Ghost Riders, with a Wild West image, and instead announced that he was thinking of changing his own name to Jim Bowie.

These eighteen months with The Konrads – he joined in

June 1962 and left on 31 December 1963 – give us a template for Bowie's early approach. Rather than trying to strike out on his own as a singer-songwriter, he worked within the existing frameworks; nudging a jobbing covers band to experiment, while pushing for his own ideas and styling the brand as much as he could. But failure is also a key aspect of Bowie's career. The Konrads' song 'I Never Dreamed' – co-written by Jones, Alan Dodds and Roger Ferris, and recorded during an audition for Decca – was rejected by the label, and the band also failed to get past the first round of Rediffusion's TV contest, *Ready, Steady, Win*. David, frustrated at his lack of control within the group, teamed up briefly again with George Underwood – significantly, their side-project the Hooker Brothers was initially called Dave's Reds and Blues, giving him top billing – and recorded music in his bedroom, using basic equipment to build guitar parts and harmonies and effectively creating a band on his own.

By January 1964, a month after leaving The Konrads, he'd recruited three older musicians, along with Underwood, into a new band, Davie Jones and The King Bees. Now he was headlining. The green corduroy, striped tie and brown mohair trousers were out, replaced by jeans, T-shirts, piratical leather waistcoats and high-cut boots from a fashionable London boutique. Acquaintances of the time describe him as 'very fashion conscious', with 'way-out clothes and dyed hair'; outrageous enough to embarrass his more conventional girlfriends.

With a distinct focus on blues, rather than just playing every chart crowd-pleaser, the King Bees had a stronger identity, and the Davie Jones of his 1964 publicity shots is more recognisable as proto-David Bowie.

Again, with characteristic inventiveness and cheek – perhaps inspired by his dad's insider knowledge – he wrote to a local entrepreneur, laundry magnate John Bloom, asking him to sponsor the band. Bloom passed the details on to talent scout Leslie Conn, who signed up David, offered the King Bees a prestigious gig and management, and negotiated a record deal with Decca. On 5 June, just six months after The Konrads' failed Decca audition, Davie Jones released his first disc, 'Liza Jane': on the 19th they performed it on Rediffusion's TV show, *Ready Steady Go!*. In July, David was fired from his job in advertising after a blazing row with his boss – he'd been working as a 'junior visualiser', a paste-up artist – or, if you believe his version of events, decided to quit and dedicate all his time to making it in the music business.

From one angle, it seems a clear-cut, focused trajectory towards his later fame. But what if The Konrads had been signed by Decca, and triumphed on *Ready, Steady, Win*? Every point of apparent failure in Bowie's 1960s is a pivot to an alternate future – now an alternate history – where his success would have come sooner, but surely would have been short-lived.

The pattern continued: a few steps forward, another

setback, and another shift. The King Bees' first major gig was a flop that left David in tears. *Juke Box Jury*, on BBC1, voted 'Liza Jane' a miss. Musically, though credited to Leslie Conn, it's indebted to the standard 'Li'l Liza Jane', and, in the words of *Rebel Rebel* author Chris O'Leary, is 'doubly derivative (aping the Stones aping American electric blues)', not far from The Konrads' straight covers. Davie Jones, despite his growing confidence, still tries to disguise his accent, though it slips through: as O'Leary notes, 'Jane' becomes a twangy 'Jayne' by the end. Anne Nightingale, in a contemporary review, called it 'straight R&B with a strong Cockney inflection'. The B-side, 'Louie, Louie Go Home', was a cover of an American release and another mash-up of borrowed styles: if the original was white kids trying to sound black, the King Bees' cover added Beatles-like backing vocals and a whiny Lennon inflection from the lead singer.

'Liza Jane' failed to sell, and David once more left the band. He was chasing success, rather than a particular sound; he even altered his accent from the A-side to the B-side of the single, as the genre shifted from blues to pop. Once again, his projects overlapped as he impatiently sought a new vehicle: he auditioned for The Manish Boys in July 1964, and quit the King Bees later that month. (But again, an alternate path branches out from this point. What if 'Liza Jane' had been a hit?)

The pattern continued into 1965. The Manish Boys recorded 'I Pity the Fool' in January and released it in March with one of David's own compositions, 'Take My Tip', on the B-side. His talent for provocation and media manipulation emerged more boldly, as he told a promoter his sexual preference was for 'boys, of course', and invented a story for the *Daily Mirror*: he'd supposedly been banned from the TV pop show *Gadzooks! It's All Happening* because of his long hair. While enjoying the press attention, David was furious that the band had persuaded Leslie Conn to drop his individual credit on the record, and release it as a single by The Manish Boys. He reasserted himself when they played at the Bromel Club, his home territory, and ensured his name was highlighted, but the other band members hit back with a reminder in their own local paper that 'Davie is a member of the group, and not, as many people think, the leader.' Again, the single tanked, and he left the band on 5 May 1965, less than a year since his audition. Once more, we get the sense that every band, every stunt, every style and soundbite was a means to an end: he wanted to cultivate his own brand, not just to join a gang.

And the cycle started again. By 17 May he was leading Davie Jones and the Lower Third. In August, the new group released 'You've Got a Habit of Leaving', credited solely to Davy Jones. It was an original composition, though this time David steered his new group towards a Who sound – built around the structure of 'Tired of Waiting for You', by The Kinks – and his vocals approximated Roger Daltrey. The

B-side, 'Baby Loves That Way', pastiches Herman's Hermits and owes a further debt to The Kinks. Drumming up attention for the new single, David met agent Ralph Horton, who agreed to manage the Lower Third and advised a style shift towards London's mod fashions.

David was still a darling of the local press – the *Kentish Times* saw it as newsworthy that 'Davie Changes His Hairstyle' – and now, under Horton's influence, adopted what the paper called a 'college-boy' look, with Carnaby Street white shirts, hipster trousers and flowery ties. In September, Horton introduced David to the more experienced manager Ken Pitt and, on Pitt's advice, they changed his stage name to Bowie. David was interviewed in style magazines – 'I consider myself just to be fashion conscious, not a mod or anything' – released 'Can't Help Thinking About Me' in early 1966 for his new label, Pye, and covertly planned to go solo. The other band members suspected, but only realised when their 29 January gig at the Bromel Club was billed as 'David Bowie', and they were told they wouldn't get paid. We can predict the next step. On 6 February, Bowie formed a new group, The Buzz, and toured with them for eight months. In August, he released 'I Dig Everything', without the band: it was his last work for Pye. Again, the writing was on the wall, and in late November, just before launching a new single on the Deram label, he told The Buzz he wouldn't be needing them in future.

The single was 'Rubber Band', with 'The London Boys' on

its B-side. 'David not only wrote the song,' boasted the press release, 'he scored the arrangement and produced the master recording.'

Finally, we've reached tracks that appear on his debut album from June 1967. It feels like a landmark: after five years of adapting, borrowing, ditching, adopting and dropping – from David Jones through Davie Jay to David Bowie, from The Konrads to The Buzz, from Pye to Deram, from Horton to Pitt – he's become the solo performer we start to recognise, grabbing his hard-hustled place on the outskirts of fame and edging closer to the centre. The LP features a close-up of his face and his stage name. He's made it, surely.

How had he got here, when so many other boys and bands from Bromley had dropped out of the race? Partly, simply, through persistence. He'd decided to make it his career, and he wanted stardom enough to get over any misgivings and hesitation. He had a safety net, certainly – not every young man can give up his job in advertising, knowing his father will fund him – but he was still pushing himself on a personal level, taking risks and forcing himself to make them come true. This had been his sole focus since the age of fourteen: or earlier, depending which story we believe.

Like a petty gangster in a crime movie, he'd kept on moving up, replacing the boss in one band then moving to a larger outfit when he got bored or felt his ambitions stifled. With every step higher, he gained more status symbols: a headline credit, a newspaper article, a TV appearance, a magazine feature. He was ruthless, self-centred, dedicated to his own success, but endearingly creative in how he achieved it. He was single-minded and canny, but also innocently imaginative: his natural shyness and sensitivity were balanced with sheer front and cheeky charm. Writing to a self-made millionaire in the laundry self-service business and asking him to sponsor the King Bees worked because it reached John Bloom out of the blue, taking the magnate by surprise. David was an artist, not a con-artist.

How much of his approach during those five years was clever media manipulation, and how much was an expression of something more personal? Were the dyed hair, piratical boots and leather blousons of 1964 the sign of David's genuine interest in way-out styling, or the fashioning of a distinctive brand image? We can't know. He may not have known himself.

We have to guess whether he was just playing with the press when he told the reporter he was into boys, 'of course', prefiguring his later claims to be gay and bisexual. We can't be sure whether he changed his hair, his clothes and brand to fit the changing market, or his own changing tastes; whether he was genuinely trying to subvert gender roles with his long hair, or whether he simply guessed it would get headlines. His interviews at the time are as frivolously playful as his later interactions with journalists: 'Insistently he claims the dubious honour of being Bromley's first "Mod" but has

since changed his philosophy to become a "Rocker",'
proclaimed his press release in 1965. David 'likes Scandinavian
"birds" . . . dislikes education, 9–5 jobs, long straight roads
and "coppers" (in either sense – "cash" or the "law")'.

Were the idiosyncratic ideas like infra-blue lighting, a Wild
West-themed band and the cartoon backdrops just an attempt
to grab attention with a gimmick, or a deeper impulse from
the boy who'd been told not to make a mess in his bedroom
with paints, and now found himself with more freedom? The
truth is that we don't have to choose – the same decision can
combine both a clever media strategy and a personal, artistic
experiment. Again, when we meet a contradiction in Bowie's
history, it doesn't always have to be resolved: we can see it
in double vision.

It's tempting to think, though, that when he dug out his
green corduroy jacket from The Konrads and drew felt-pen
stripes over it, customising it for his brief role with the Riot
Squad in spring 1967, that this was an act of individual
expression, a creative sabotage of the uniform he'd worn in
his first band. In contrast to the teenage investment he'd put
into The Konrads, the Riot Squad was a deliberately short-
term fling for a twenty-year-old Bowie. The band knew he
was going to move on, and they welcomed his ideas of hand-
painted props, mime and make-up: they already used a
flashing blue police light in performances, which may have
drawn him in. He even hid behind a disguise rather than

using his real (stage) name, adopting the temporary alias 'Toy Soldier' in promotional material: perhaps his first persona. The jacket is now on display in Bromley Library, one floor down from the maps and local directories. 'It's tiny, isn't it?' the archivist remarked to me. 'And what a conservative type of rebellion' – she laughed – 'to draw pinstripes on your own jacket!'

He'd been writing his own lyrics since at least summer 1962; The Konrads backing singer Stella Gall remembers him noting them down in an exercise book. He didn't have to persuade a band to let him perform them now, or compete for credit. He no longer had to cover this week's hits, or ape the sound of Lennon and The Beatles, or Daltrey and The Who. This was his opportunity to let the world hear David Bowie. What did he do with his new solo platform? He let the world hear another Anthony Newley.

That's an over-simplification, of course. But Bowie's debut album for Deram is a compilation of oddities, made up largely of short stories about quirky characters: a 'Little Bombardier' who is driven out of town for inappropriate friendships with children; 'Uncle Arthur' who leaves his wife and returns to Mother's cooking; the cross-dressing soldier in 'She's Got Medals'. These are vignettes with a mild twist, centring veterans from wars before Bowie's time – the narrator of 'Rubber Band' fought in the 1914–18 conflict – and delivered with a chirpy-chappy vocal. The sound effects and melodramatic acting of 'Please Mr Gravedigger', the spoken punchlines at the end of 'Rubber Band' and 'Love You Till Tuesday', and the comedy voices (Nazis, news announcers) on 'We Are Hungry Men' add to the sense of vaudeville. Like 'Rubber Band', 'Maid of Bond Street' is based around a play on words ('this girl is made of lipstick . . . this girl is maid of Bond Street'), and 'She's Got Medals' also does double-service as a dirty joke, as Chris O'Leary points out (basically, 'she's got balls').

O'Leary suggests that Bowie's shift towards music-hall pastiche and a celebration of an imaginary English past was a clever move, 'acutely timed' to fit with a nostalgic 1967 trend for brigadier moustaches and military uniforms. The brass-buttoned jacket Bowie wears on the LP's cover is a smart, sober version of The Beatles' multicoloured *Sgt. Pepper* get-up; their album, celebrating a mythical military band that launched 'twenty years ago today', was released the same week as Bowie's. On the other hand, we know that Bowie had genuinely been inspired by Newley back in 1961, before he joined The Konrads, and may have seen this shift into theatrical storytelling as a way to express himself as an original artist; a sharp about-turn from the stale Mod scene.

On one level, we shouldn't expect Bowie's 1960s solo work to tell us anything about his upbringing and environment. His decisions so far had all been based around gaining greater independence and celebrity, using each band in turn to move further away from the Bromley music scene. His gigs took him on increasingly wider circuits, from school fêtes and local village halls with The Konrads in 1963, to the Jack of Clubs and the Marquee in Soho with The King Bees in 1964, to gigs in Maidstone, Newcastle and Edinburgh with The Manish Boys by the end of that year. In December 1965 and January 1966, he performed with the Lower Third at Le Golf-Drouot and Le Bus Palladium in Paris.

But on the other hand, he kept returning: not just to Soho – he held a regular slot at the Marquee Club – but to the Bromel Club, barely fifteen minutes' walk from his parents' home. He was still living at Plaistow Grove in 1965, though he shuttled between Bromley and Maidstone during his stint with The Manish Boys, and spent nights in between gigs at friends' houses or in the band's van. As a minor, Bowie still needed his parents to sign his contracts, and drew a sketch map for Pitt in summer 1966, showing him how to get from Sundridge Park Station to 4 Plaistow Grove: Pitt wrote to John Jones and 'your wife' to confirm that he would be David's sole manager, and visited Bromley in February 1967 to go through the paperwork. The first time Bowie formally moved out from his parents' house was June of that year, when he began sharing Pitt's apartment in London; even then, he only spent Monday to Friday with Pitt, and went back to Bromley at weekends. He unashamedly told a magazine in July of that year that he still lived at home with his parents. 'I'd never leave them; we've got a good thing going.' As O'Leary points out 'The London Boys', despite its edgy urban setting, was written by a teenager 'living in Bromley, fed and clothed and funded by his parents', and feels like 'a suburban correspondent filing a story from the field'.

Though part of him was trying to escape his background, he was clearly reluctant to fully give it up, and this tension crept into his work, sometimes between the lines and sometimes more explicitly. Bromley was the territory he knew best, and it formed part of his mental landscape. But what emerges more strongly is a sense of in-betweenness: the dynamic between safety and escape, comfort and frustration, home and adventure, city and suburb, family and freedom. Bowie's first-person narrators and characters of the period are often caught between these choices, poised in limbo.

Take, for instance, 'Can't Help Thinking About Me' (January 1966), which Kevin Cann sees as a 'confessional and reflective' evocation of 'his mother, Sundridge Park Station, the recreation ground at the end of his street, St Mary's Church'. While it lends itself to an autobiographical reading, with a girl calling out, 'Hi, Dave,' its lyrics are, in fact, not nearly so specific as Cann suggests – there's a church, a mother, a recreation ground, a station and indeed a school, but they are left generic. The song focuses on the moment when its young narrator is forced to leave ('I've gotta pack my bags, leave this home'), revisits memories of the home town as he walks to the station, and ends at a point of transition, while 'the ticket's in my hand'. His family and friends are left behind in 'never-never land', but his future is unknown: 'I've got a long way to go, hope I make it on my own.'

'The London Boys' (December 1966) finds its central character a few steps down the line, but equally uncertain. 'You moved away, told your folks you were gonna stay away.' This protagonist is 'seventeen, but you think you've grown, in the month you've been away from your parents' home'; like the narrator of 'Can't Help Thinking About Me', he's traded comfort for uncertainty, and now can't turn back. 'It's too late now, cause you're out there boy . . . now you wish you'd never left your home, you've got what you wanted but you're on your own.'

'I Dig Everything' (August 1966) checks in on the same milieu on a different day, in a more upbeat mood. The newcomer in 'The London Boys' has bought coffee, butter and bread but 'can't make a thing cause the meter's dead'; in 'I Dig Everything', the narrator 'ain't had a job for a year or more', rents 'a backstreet room in the back part of town', and is 'low on money . . . everything's spent', but he doesn't care – he feeds the lions in Trafalgar Square, makes friends with the time-check girl on the end of the phone, and waves to policemen. He finds stuff to do for free. He digs everything. He's made himself a home in London. Even so, the joy in this song stems from uncertainty ('I don't know a thing'), and from embracing the precarious balance between success and failure ('some of them were losers but the rest of them are winners').

Bowie's debut album moves away from this semi-autobiographical approach – two of the examples above are from a first-person perspective, and have 'I' and 'Me' in their titles – but uses the same dynamic structures with some of the character vignettes. The 'Little Bombardier', like the narrator in 'Can't Help Thinking About Me', is thrown out of his home town and catches a train towards an uncertain future; though the tone tends towards throwaway comedy rather than teenage angst, the ending is almost identical.

'Uncle Arthur', finally, is still living with Mother, facing 'another empty day' of routine tedium as the bell strikes five and he closes the family shop; he finds romance late in life, at age thirty-two, but runs back to Mummy when he realises his new bride can't cook. By contrast, 'The London Boys' opens with Bow Bells striking another night, and its protagonist returning wearily to seedy digs without electricity. Both options – living with your mum in cossetted security into your thirties ('he gets his pocket money, he's well fed'), and scrounging for food and friends as a seventeen-year-old in Soho – are presented as imperfect. Arthur experiments with freedom and quickly abandons it; the 'London Boy' pretends he's having fun, but secretly regrets that he can't go home. Even in their vaudeville disguise, then, Bowie's songs from

1967 work through his own experiences as a young man who'd toured widely with bands and secured a regular gig at a club in Soho, but kept returning to his home base in Bromley; a solo artist who still needed his dad's signature, who depended on his parents for support, and who couldn't seem fully to get away from the street where he'd grown up.

But all this was behind him now. It was June 1967, and he had a solo record out, with his name and face on the cover. He'd made it, surely.

He hadn't made it. The singles, 'Rubber Band' and 'Love You Till Tuesday', flopped, and the album tanked at 125 in the UK charts. Another possible future for Bowie closed down: as Chris O'Leary suggests, 'Love You Till Tuesday' was a strong enough contender in the lacklustre music market of summer 1967 to have reached the top ten. With a successful follow-up, O'Leary speculates, it could have led to an alternate path of cabaret, Vegas shows, duets with Petula Clark and Nancy Sinatra, Bacharach covers and a disco crossover hit in the 1970s. That Bowie remains in a parallel universe, with all the other what-ifs and might-have-beens.

He was dropped by Deram the following year. The experience would surely have destroyed the confidence and drive of many twenty-year-old artists: he'd had his shot, and the world didn't want to listen. Instead, he branched out into other fields. Some of his attempts were rewarded with small success; most were met with failure, but still he kept going.

Bowie kept busy over the next eighteen months. He had what Ken Pitt called, in a letter to John Jones, a 'very brave try' at writing the music for Zeffirelli's *Romeo and Juliet*: the director chose Donovan instead. He took up mime and movement with Lindsay Kemp, who has variously described his protégé as both 'a joy to direct . . . an ideal student' and, more recently, 'a load of shit'. Bowie performed in Kemp's stage play *Pierrot in Turquoise*, and explored Buddhism, professing that he hoped, at age twenty-five, 'to be in Tibet studying Eastern philosophy . . . money doesn't mean all that much to me.' He auditioned unsuccessfully for musicals and feature films and won a role in a short called *The Image*, followed by a tiny cameo in *The Virgin Soldiers*. He sent a television play to the BBC and had it rejected; to placate his dad, who was worried about his son's career, he tried a cabaret act, which came to nothing. One booking agent advised Ken Pitt: 'Let him have a good day job . . . he's never going to get anywhere.' Instead, Bowie started his own dance and mime group, Feathers, with his new girlfriend Hermione Farthingale and his friend Tony 'Hutch' Hutchinson. 'He'd try one thing, try another,' Hermione later remembered. 'He wasn't lost. He just wasn't found, either.' He never stopped trying; but he didn't release any records during 1968.

In early 1969 the relationship with Hermione ended, and Bowie moved back to Plaistow Grove, briefly, for the final time. He filmed a commercial for Luv ice lollies: the advert performed so badly that the product was taken off the market. With Pitt's encouragement, Bowie shot his own promotional film, *Love You Till Tuesday*, going to the trouble of getting cosmetic work on his teeth, and wearing hairpieces to disguise his *Virgin Soldiers* short back and sides. Costs escalated, and experimental sections were scrapped. When the film was finished, Pitt arranged private screenings: TV stations and film distributors were unmoved. The project was shelved; but as part of its production, Bowie had written a new song, 'Space Oddity'.

Once more, we reach a point of recognition. Surely, now, Bowie has done it. This is the hit single we all know. This is the brink of fame. 'Space Oddity' would open the album most of us recognise as his first – it was also named *David Bowie* – after the false start of the Deram LP. Bowie himself, typically, wrote his debut out of history, claiming in a 1972 interview that 'I was still working as a commercial artist then and I made it in my spare time, taking days off work and all that. I never followed it up . . . sent my tape into Decca and they said they'd make an album.' According to the popular myth of Bowie, this is the real beginning. It's worth freeze-framing him again here, and asking how he reached this point, after the crashing failure of 1967. How did he get past the disappointment, and retain his drive? Why did he keep trying?

We can only speculate, while acknowledging that every decision can have several motivations: a need to live up to

Ken Pitt's expectations and investment; perhaps a desire to please his dad, who, as Bowie told an interviewer in 1968, 'tries so hard' and still supported him; certainly, Bowie seemed to retain an almost untouchable core of self-belief. In a conversation with George Tremlett in 1969, he explained, 'smiling but firm', that 'I shall be a millionaire by the time I'm thirty.' Tremlett comments that 'by the way he said it, I saw the possibility that he might not make it had barely crossed his mind.' There is another possible reason, concealed within the frantic comedy of 'The Laughing Gnome', his single from 1967. This novelty song failed to make it onto the Deram LP, was reviewed at the time as 'the flop it deserved to be', and haunted Bowie's subsequent career. Understandably, it remained part of the 1960s he'd rather forget.

But while its high-pitched vocals and Christmas-cracker jokes make it an even broader music-hall number than 'Uncle Arthur', it shares intriguingly similar motifs with Bowie's other work of the time: a local high street, a quirky older character, threats of authority ('I ought to report you to the Gnome Office'), and forced exile via the railway station ('I put him on a train to Eastbourne'). The narrator in 'Can't Help Thinking About Me' leaves his family in 'never-never land', and sets out towards an uncertain future, 'on my own'; the gnome is asked, 'haven't you got a home to go to,' and replies that he's from 'gnome-man's land', a 'gnome-ad'. Like the 'London Boy' and 'Uncle Arthur', the gnome is drawn back from his wandering towards suburbia and home comforts: when the narrator puts him on a train to the coast, he appears again next morning, bringing his brother. Even the references to success, described in terms of eating well ('living on caviar and honey, cause they're earning me lots of money') echo the rhyming contrasts between family security and precarious independence in 'Uncle Arthur' and 'The London Boys' ('he gets his pocket money, he's well fed'; 'you've bought some coffee, butter and bread, you can't make a thing cause the meter's dead.') Behind the frenetic gags, 'The Laughing Gnome' explores the same tension as Bowie's more anguished singles from the same period: the push and pull of comforting, dull safety versus risky adventure. The same dynamic recurs, more metaphorically, throughout his later work, and can even be seen to structure Bowie's career; we'll return to it later. Already, though, we can see that this song has more to it than meets the eye.

It's easy to dismiss 'The Laughing Gnome' as a convenient vehicle for packing in as many gnome jokes as possible. But as we've already seen, Bowie was tempted by puns in his more serious tracks, too. 'Rubber Band' may be frivolous, but 'Maid of Bond Street', also built around a play on words, isn't meant to be funny. 'Space Oddity' followed – ostensibly spoofing *2001: A Space Odyssey* (the name 'David Bowie' even sounds like a parody riff on the movie's protagonist, Dave Bowman) but far from a comedy song – and then 'Aladdin

Sane', containing the hidden confession 'A Lad Insane'. The cover of *Low* is a visual joke on 'low profile'. 'New Killer Star', from 2003, puns on George W. Bush's pronunciation of 'nuclear', but the song is no joke: it opens with a reflection on the 'great white scar' of the former World Trade Center.

In 1997, Bowie returned self-consciously to 'grumpy gnomes' with 'Little Wonder', which includes the names of the Seven Dwarves in its lyrics and has a twist in its title: depending on context, the phrase is used to imply both 'no wonder, then', and 'you little marvel'. Linguistic gags in Bowie's work are not, then, a cue for us to disregard the song as meaningless cabaret. In fact, the hysterical surplus of double meaning in 'The Laughing Gnome' could even be seen as an invitation to read more into the lyrics, like a dream bursting with symbolism that begs for analysis. 'Gnomic', after all, also signifies a mysterious expression of truth, and leads us, in turn, to Bowie's description for the mousy-haired girl in 'Life on Mars'. In a 2008 article he called her an 'anomic (not a "gnomic") heroine'. He knew the word could be read in other ways.

If we accept that the song can be taken more seriously, then the gnome's brother, who appears at the end of the narrator's bed one morning, is the key to further interpretation. David Jones had, more than once, woken up to find his half-brother, Terry, back from his nomadic travels and sharing his bedroom. Terry was ten when he first joined the Jones family at Stansfield Road in Brixton; but when they moved to Bromley in 1953, Terry, who hated John Jones, stayed behind. In June 1955 he came back, taking the bedroom next to David's on Plaistow Grove; in November, he left again for the air force, and didn't return for three years. He couldn't stay, Peggy explained when Terry turned up again, unkempt and disturbed – the back bedrooms had been merged into one, and there was no room – so he moved out to Forest Hill, but still caught the bus regularly to Bromley, to visit David. Terry was already a major influence on his younger half-brother, helping him, as Peter and Leni Gillman put it, to 'discover a new world beyond the drab confines of the suburbs'. He took David to jazz clubs in Soho, gave him a copy of Kerouac's *On the Road*, and encouraged him towards saxophone lessons. 'I thought the world of David,' he later said, 'and he thought the world of me.' An intermittent resident at Plaistow Grove over the next decade, Terry was also in and out of local hospitals for the mentally ill. He was developing schizophrenia.

In February 1967, David and Terry – now both adults – walked down to the Bromel Club to see Cream in concert. 'I was very disturbed,' Bowie later recalled, 'because the music was affecting him adversely. His particular illness was some-where between schizophrenia and manic depressiveness . . . I remember having to take him home.' According to Buckley's biography, Terry 'began pawing the road' after the gig.

'He could see cracks in the tarmac and flames rising up, as if from the underworld. Bowie was scared witless . . . this example of someone so close being possessed was horrifying.' He was, Buckley goes on, 'frightened that his own mind would split down the middle, too'. Bowie's own recollection is, as we've seen, less melodramatic, but he confirmed in another interview, with a formality that suggests he was choosing his words carefully, that 'one puts oneself through such psychological damage trying to avoid the threat of insanity, you start to approach the very thing that you're scared of. Because of the tragedy inflicted, especially on my mother's side . . . that was something I was terribly fearful of.' His grandmother, Margaret, had also suffered from mental illness, as had his aunts Una, Nora and Vivienne; Terry's episode at the Bromel Club brought it closer to home, though it's worth noting that cousin Kristina dismissed Terry's experience as a 'bad acid trip', and the idea of insanity in the family as one of David's long-term lies, or 'porkies'. 'It just wasn't true,' she told Francis Whately in 2019.

Terry features obliquely in at least two of Bowie's songs. 'Jump They Say' (1993), Bowie explained, was 'semi-based on my impression of my stepbrother'; he was cagier about 'The Bewlay Brothers' (1971), throwing out various decoy explanations before admitting, in 1977, that it was about himself and Terry, with 'Bewlay' as an echo of his own stage name. 'The Laughing Gnome' is never discussed in this context

– it is, at best, accepted by critics as a bit of fun, or in the words of Peter and Leni Gillman, 'a delightful children's record' – but it's tempting to add it to the list of songs inspired by Bowie's half-brother, especially if we bear in mind a story that Kristina tells about Terry and their grandmother. Little Terry had nervously smiled after being scolded. 'Nanny said, "Go on, laugh again," and he smirked again, and she smacked him across the ear and said, "That'll teach you to laugh at me."' Ha ha ha. Hee hee hee.

It's a persuasive reading. But to label 'The Laughing Gnome' with a single interpretation – a song about Terry Burns, the manic outsider who kept turning up at David's house, and was sent away – would be reductive. Any Bowie song is, like the man who wrote it, a matrix of information, with multiple possible patterns of connection. Even single words can be loaded, and can pivot in various directions, suggesting different links. We can join the dots of those words and phrases in several ways and create a convincing structure, but with a twist, and from a new perspective, the picture changes. As I've suggested, 'The Laughing Gnome' also explores Bowie's to-and-fro tension between independent adventure and the security of home. It's also, let's face it, a comedy song, a novelty number, a 'delightful children's record'. It can be all those things and more. An interview with novelist Hanif Kureishi gives a further quick twist and suggests a final angle.

Kureishi recalls that, when they worked on *Buddha of Suburbia* together, Bowie 'would talk about how awkward it was in the house for his mother and father when Terry was around, how difficult and disturbing it was'. But he immediately goes on, without changing the subject, to describe his own experiences with Bowie on the phone. 'I got the sense you have with some psychotic people when they're just talking to themselves. It's just a monologue, and he is just sharing with you what's going round and round in his head.' From Terry's schizophrenia to David's seeming psychosis, without a jump: the seamless segue is telling, and it's a short step from there to Chris O'Leary's suggestion that 'The Laughing Gnome' is 'a man losing his mind, a schizophrenic's conversation with himself'.

It would seem overly simplistic to suggest that Bowie channelled a fear of insanity directly into his work – 'All the Madmen' (1970), for instance, or the 'crack in the sky and the hand reaching down to me' from 'Oh! You Pretty Things' (1971) – unless he'd admitted it himself. 'I felt I was the lucky one because I was an artist and it would never happen to me because I could put all my psychological excesses into my music and then I could be always throwing it off.' This confession, included in Dylan Jones's book, follows directly on from the quotation above ('one puts oneself through such psychological damage...'). Note how Bowie's formal poise switches into a rushed incantation;

an attempt to make something true by saying it quickly.

In this sense, then, 'The Laughing Gnome' is not just about Terry, but about what Terry meant to his younger half-brother: a troubled alter-ego who always comes back when he's sent away, a reminder of what Bowie could have been, and what he feared he could still become. The laughing gnome is a figure embodying both madness and truth: manic laughter and gnomic warnings. You can't catch him, and you can't get away from him. He can't be successfully repressed, but he can be accepted and embraced, not just peaceably but profitably ('we're living on caviar and honey, cause they're earning me lots of money'). If we follow this interpretation to its conclusion, Bowie was not just pushing himself because he hungered for fame. He was driven to keep creating because he wanted to expel the ideas from his head into his art; he preferred to make the hallucination into a comedy character, rather than hear that high-pitched chuckling confined to his own head. He wanted to exorcise the energy before it could drive him crazy. He felt his art would save him, and perhaps it did; as the song predicts, it certainly earned him success.

Was his creative drive really fuelled, at least in part, by this fear of mental illness? We can't be sure: we can only try to read back through Bowie's public art into his private motivations, using the facts of his life as a framework. But it's a valid way of seeing, and it makes a good story.

Bowie kept trying, despite all the setbacks, and kept working, and kept moving. After another brief stay at Plaistow Grove in January 1969, he'd relocated to 24 Foxgrove Road in Beckenham, which he shared with Barrie Jackson, a childhood friend from his old street. The following month he moved in with Mary Finnigan, in the ground-floor flat of the same house. His relationship with Finnigan quickly changed from neighbours to lovers, and then adapted again when he met Angie Barnett on Wednesday 9 April. In August, David and Angie moved to Haddon Hall, at 42 Southend Road, Beckenham, where they rented the entire ground floor of a Victorian villa.

Both Haddon Hall and 24 Foxgrove Road have been demolished and replaced with flats. You can still visit both sites, though, and realise how close they are to each other; Foxgrove Road is five minutes up the hill from Beckenham Junction Station, and 42 Southend Road less than ten minutes' further walk in the same direction. Beckenham Junction, in turn, is just two stops down the line from Bromley. Again, Bowie's sense of adventure, experiment and escape was tempered with caution. He'd moved out of his parents' home, and in with a neighbour from his childhood street; he then relocated downstairs with Mary Finnigan, making friends with her young children and becoming part of a new family household.

When he finally rented his own place with a long-term girl-friend, he was still only a couple of miles from his childhood home; easily close enough for his mother to come round and prepare Sunday lunches for Bowie and his friends. Peggy later moved to a flat in Beckenham, even nearer to her adult son, and when Bowie and Angie married, they held the ceremony at Bromley Register Office, with the reception in the Swan and Mitre pub. However, while Haddon Hall was only a few miles from Plaistow Grove, it was a world away from the tiny terraced house where David had grown up: a gothic playground with a grand piano, stained-glass windows, heavy oak and crushed velvet upholstery. Bowie and Angie would go out to clubs together and bring dates back; band members slept on mattresses across the landing, and the basement was converted into a rehearsal studio.

Finally, he'd found what he'd been working towards. His former lover Mary had made friends with his new girlfriend Angie; he invited his friend, producer Tony Visconti, to move in with them. Together, David and Mary Finnigan developed an Arts Lab at the Three Tuns, down the hill on Beckenham High Street. Bowie was the star act, backed by psychedelic liquid light shows, and the audience reached over two hundred during the summer. They organised an open-air festival for the same day as Woodstock, at Croydon Road Recreation Ground (the bandstand is still there). Bowie started to record a new album in July, and released 'Space Oddity' as a single on 11 July, in time to catch the buzz around the moon landing. John Jones wrote to Ken Pitt that 'David is keeping very cheerful and seems to be keeping himself fully occupied.' It was summer 1969. After seven years of trying, Bowie had made it.

But there was another heavy blow in his step-by-step progress towards greater independence. His move into Haddon Hall immediately followed the death of John Jones, at age fifty-six, on 5 August. Bowie had just returned from a festival in Malta, and had come back in time to perform at the Arts Lab. Mary Finnigan informed him after the set that his father was seriously ill, and Bowie arrived at Plaistow Grove to find him semi-conscious. He struggled through the Free Festival, in what he understandably called 'one of my terrible moods'. Later, he explained that he'd lost his father 'at a point where I was just beginning to grow up a little bit and appreciate that I would have to stretch out my hand a little for us ever to get to know each other. He just died at the wrong damn time . . .'

'Space Oddity' started slowly in the chart, then rose to number 25, earning Bowie his first appearance on *Top of the Pops* in early October. The single reached number 5 at the start of November, the perfect lead-in to his second album on Friday 14 of that month. With a youthful mixture of humility and arrogance, Bowie told the *NME*, 'I've been the male equivalent of a dumb blonde for a few years, and I was beginning to despair of people accepting me for my music.

It may be fine for a male model to be told he's a great looking guy but that doesn't help a singer much.' In early 1970 he formed a new band, the Hype, teaming up for the first time with guitarist Mick Ronson and drummer Woody Woodmansey. The team we know as the Spiders from Mars was almost entirely in place, adopting larger-than-life stage personae ('Spaceman', 'Hypeman', 'Gangsterman'): with hindsight, it looks like the start of glam rock. And then in March 1970 Bowie released his follow-up to 'Space Oddity', 'The Prettiest Star'. It sold 798 copies and died. He wouldn't have another hit single for two years. He hadn't made it after all.

I sat in the Zizzi on Beckenham High Street, which is now decorated with a mural of Bowie and key quotations from his songs in the windows. At the next table, three teenage lads ordered bashfully from a blonde waitress, in front of the lyrics 'When you're a boy, you can wear a uniform; when you're a boy, other boys check you out.' Fifty years ago, Bowie sat here with his acoustic guitar, playing for a crowd of regulars. This Zizzi was the Three Tuns until 1995, then the Rat and Parrot. In 2001, Mary Finnigan and supporters installed a plaque celebrating the Arts Lab and anticipating that the pub's former name would be restored: it was, but only for a year. The plaque is still out front, with its perhaps overambitious boast that Bowie launched his career here; a Three Tuns sign hangs alongside the Zizzi logo.

It's hard to know the truth about any period in Bowie's

life. Some stories are built on more solid foundations, and some are shakier. The popular idea that Bowie shocked the world in the early 1970s as a fully-formed genius makes him easier to idolise, perhaps, but harder to aspire to, and harder to identify with. It is easier to treat him as a creature of uncanny talent, an unearthly one-off, because it erases the years of struggle behind his success and allows us to think of him as different to the rest of us. But in many ways, he wasn't different to the rest of us. He wasn't trained as a singer. He didn't show early signs of musical ability. He was an uncertain frontman as a teenager, insecure about his own vocal abilities. You can hear him improving from single to single during the 1960s. He taught himself saxophone at the age of fifteen, learning to play along with his favourite records, and focused on it while he was convalescing from his eye injury: he took lessons, but only from spring until summer 1962. He could pick out chords on a guitar and piano, but couldn't read or write music; he used descriptions in a book to choose the instruments for his debut album, and relied on colour-coded charts, instead of conventional notation, for 'Space Oddity'. As a dancer, an artist and an actor he was an enthusiastic amateur. He had the privileges of being a white, lower-middle-class teenager in a little house in a safe neighbourhood; but he also had to deal with a troubled half-brother who clashed with his parents, a family history of mental illness and the early loss of his father.

In September 1972, David Jones sailed with his wife Angie to New York on the *QE2*. He was now not just David Bowie, but Ziggy Stardust, complete with the crimson hair, jumpsuits and platform boots. They checked into the Plaza Hotel on Central Park and went up to their suite. 'Babe,' said Angie – or so the story goes – as she looked around at the decor, the view and the gifts from the production company, 'we've made it.'

He'd made it, finally. But it was now ten years since David Jones had joined The Konrads and played Shadows covers at the Royal Bell in Bromley: ten years of false starts, frustrations and failures. Yes, Bowie was exceptional, but part of what distinguished him from all the other boys in bands, in Bromley 1962 – and the only reason we've heard of him at all – was his refusal to give up in those early days. The story matters because Bowie showed us, among other things, what an ordinary person can become, with enough tenacity and self-belief. It took him ten years. If you started now, where could you be in a decade?

2

CONNECTING

Like most Bowie fans, I find his song titles and lyrics popping regularly into my head, framing my thought patterns and commenting on what I'm doing, like comic-book captions. You'll have your own personal selection of phrases and sound-bites. One of mine is from 'Five Years'. In the second verse, his head reeling from the news of impending apocalypse, Bowie finds himself assaulted by the sounds of telephones, opera houses and favourite songs, seeing 'boys, toys, electric irons and TVs. My brain hurt like a warehouse,' he wails. 'It had no room to spare; I had to cram so many things to store everything in there.' The line hooks in my head not just because it describes so many of Bowie's lyrics, but because it captures the way his greatest songs make me feel: crammed with ideas and energy.

We're immersed again in this sense of crowded, overflowing impressions in 'Life on Mars?', with its pull back from cavemen, sailors and lawmen to a dreamscape geography that roams from America to Ibiza to the Norfolk Broads, starring Mickey Mouse and his hordes, Lennon (or possibly Lenin) and 'my mother'. There's a hypnotic, almost robotic stream of information in 'Looking for Satellites', with its chanted litany of commercial images: nowhere, shampoo, TV, combat, Boy's Own, slim tie, showdown. 'Can't stop,' Bowie intones, before beginning the list again. These mixed-up fragments are, to an extent, the result of Bowie's experimental approach to writing, which in the 1970s included improvised composition at the mic and cutting up song-words with scissors, and in the 1990s used a laptop program called the Verbasizer to randomise sentences. But they also speak to his hunger for information, and his impatience – again, particularly during the 1970s and the mid-1990s – for new challenges, new genres, new prompts and provocations.

His lyrics are typically packed with references: passing nods, brief quotations and half-hidden echoes. If we follow his leads, tracing them back towards their sources, we can learn more about him; but we can also, as he did, simply learn more, for the sake of it. And as we follow each lead further back, with each reference splitting and branching, taking us beyond the source and beyond Bowie's intentions, we learn more again: about the world, and perhaps also about ourselves.

I'm a Bowie fan, but also a professor of cultural studies; and so the image of a brain like a warehouse, with no room to spare, reminds me of concepts from academic theory. The anthropologist Victor Turner, for instance, describes liminality, or the state of in-betweenness, as 'fructile chaos, a fertile nothingness, a storehouse of possibilities, not by any means a random assemblage but a striving after new forms and structure, a gestation process'. Words and phrases leap out of this passage, linking up with Bowie's imagery: chaos, a storehouse, a warehouse with no room. We can jump back and forward between his lyrics and Turner's theory, joining the dots.

In 'Looking for Satellites', the narrator announces that we are 'nowhere': 'where do we go from here?' he wonders, scanning the sky. 'There's nothing in our eyes; as lonely as a moon, misty and far away.' It's an expression of emptiness, but, as in Turner's account, the nothingness is fertile: from this isolation comes a feed of images, channelled through Bowie as if he's the satellite receiver. Shampoo. TV. Combat. Boy's Own. (Or Boyzone – Bowie denied the pun, but that doesn't stop us from hearing a double meaning.) As listeners, we try to make sense of this list, 'striving after new forms and structure' rather than dismissing it as 'random assemblage'.

Turner's description, then, can help us to understand how we construct meaning from Bowie's flow of fragmented phrases, and transform them from a chaos of possibilities into a new understanding. We take part in the process, helping the song to 'gestate', giving the words a logical framework and forming them into a more solid shape. The songs change through our personal interpretation, which is why your 'Life on Mars?' – like your 'Looking for Satellites' and your 'Five Years' – will be different from mine. (On the simplest level, if you hear 'Lennon' and 'Boyzone' instead of 'Lenin' and 'Boy's Own', the pictures in your head will be very different.) We fill in the gaps between his fragments in different ways, investing them with our own experiences and imagination. Of course, Turner wasn't talking about David Bowie, and that doesn't matter. Academic theory is a tool that can be used outside its original context, to open up and illuminate our everyday lives.

From Bowie's crowded warehouse and Turner's storehouse of possibilities, my mind leaps sideways to the exhibits of the international *David Bowie Is* exhibition – perhaps the closest we'll get to wandering through his subconscious – and the studio of his 'Where Are We Now?' video from 2013, crammed with souvenirs and projections of the past.

I think of other theorists, from different fields, whose imagery intersects and connects. Fredric Jameson describes postmodern culture as an 'imaginary museum' in which we can only 'imitate dead styles' and 'speak through the masks and with the voices of the styles': a museum is, after all, another kind of warehouse, full of historical costumes and props. From there, I remember another theorist with a similar metaphor. Mikhail Bakhtin suggests that literature is a kind of 'castle', filled with 'the traces of centuries and generations . . . arranged in it in visible form as various parts of its architecture, in furnishings, weapons, the ancestral portrait gallery, the family archives'. To Bakhtin, fiction itself is filled with 'isolated curiosities and rarities . . . self-sufficient items – curious, odd, wondrous . . . congealed "suddenlys", adventures turned into things'. A warehouse, a storehouse, a museum, a castle full of curiosities and rarities: these three theorists have all, in their different contexts, drawn on similar images that overlap and echo, rebounding off each other in their own chamber of ideas, and suggesting new angles on Bowie's work.

My first Bowie album was 1983's *Let's Dance*, which to me was a soundtrack for imaginary films. I visualised cinematic love scenes with 'Criminal World' as the swoony, classy backing music – I was thirteen, after all – and action sequences edited to 'Cat People'. The spoken introduction to 'Modern Love' – Bowie's gruff 'I know when to go out. I know when to stay in. Get things done' – sounded like a sample from a TV drama; the opening voiceover from a gritty British detective. But it was 'Ricochet', the challenging, art-rock track that opened side B, that really gripped me. *March of flowers! March of dimes!* As I hinted in the introduction, I knew it had to mean something; something sophisticated that I didn't yet understand. (And in a way it did: the March of Dimes is a real organisation founded by President Roosevelt, though if 'march of flowers' has another, deeper significance, it still escapes me.)

'Ricochet', to me, opened up worlds. It filled my warehouse-head with ideas, and I made my own sense of them. An accented voice, distorted by static, recited weary reports of workers who struggled off to the gates before the sun, and even at night dreamed of 'tramlines, factories, pieces of machinery, mineshafts, things like that'. In villages overshad-owed by industry, parents turned the holy pictures to the wall, as warnings blared out from media preachers and their backing choirs. *Sound of thunder! Sound of gold! Sound of the devil breaking parole!* 'Ricochet' sketches a fable of oppression and resistance through a scattering of vivid domestic details and spoken confessionals, interrupted by the chanted slogans of political and religious rhetoric. Despite the relentless drum-beats and doomy pronouncements – 'these are the prisons, these are the crimes, teaching life in a violent new way' – the song is punctuated with an upbeat shout of reassurance. 'Ricochet! It's not the end of the world.'

I still don't know what it was meant to mean, but I know what it meant to me. The ideas gathered in my brain and spilled out, leading me down my own creative paths beyond the song itself. I created characters based on 'Ricochet' – it sounded like a superhero, the codename for a future cop or teenage rebel – and wrote stories and scripts, drawing logos and costume designs. (I even imagined how my hero 'Ricochet' would dress, and on a trip to Lewisham Shopping Centre bought the jacket closest to the one in my head.) I don't believe I would have studied poetry at school with anything like the same enthusiasm if Bowie's lyrics hadn't made me feel that unlocking the meaning of enigmatic words and phrases could be a form of investigation, a fascinating process of detection. In a way, it was an important point on the route that took me into academia and brought me here.

Let's Dance isn't everyone's favourite (or first) Bowie album, but however you originally encountered him, you may have had the same experience. If you came to Bowie in 1993, for instance, there was 'Strangers When We Meet', on *Buddha of Suburbia*, with its cosmopolitan references to 'no trendy *rechauffé* . . . humming Rheingold, we trade by *vendu*'. The song appears again on *1. Outside* (1995), where you could also ponder over the passing mentions of architects Philip Johnson and Richard Rogers. During the 'Berlin' period, you could have dreamed cities from the soundscapes of 'Warszawa' (*Low*), with its haunting, almost decipherable calls in an invented language (*'Sula vie dilejo; solo vie milejo'*). At the end of *Hunky Dory*, from 1971, there's the riddling story of 'The Bewlay Brothers', also known as the 'moon boys' and the 'Kings of Oblivion': one brother was stone, and one, more malleable, was wax, a 'chameleon, comedian, Corinthian and caricature'.

In 2016, of course, Bowie left us with the last puzzles of 'Lazarus' and 'Blackstar', a final message told across two enigmatic videos: a jewelled skull in an astronaut helmet, a villa of Ormen, a dying man with bandaged eyes, and a manic double wearing the striped shirt from Bowie's far earlier *Station to Station* album. 'Station to Station' itself, from 1976, is loaded with occult images, invoking the Tree of Life (another kind of map, or matrix) as it branches 'from Kether to Malkuth'. Even the seemingly simple rocker 'Janine', on Bowie's second LP from 1969, includes evocative word-choices – 'your strange demand to collocate my mind' – and images that prefigure the more obviously complex 'Ashes to Ashes': 'if you take an axe to me you'll kill another man, not me at all.'

We don't need to know that Franz Kafka wrote: 'a book must be the axe for the frozen sea inside us,' to have our imagination struck and sparked by that sudden image in 'Janine'. We don't have to understand the Tree of Life, and the relative positions of Kether and Malkuth (crown and kingdom, respectively) to feel the power of the evocation in 'Station to Station'. We don't need to know that Ormen is also a town in Norway, and that the word translates as 'serpent', to be captured by the opening words of 'Lazarus'; we don't need to remember that Bowie wore a 'Song of Norway' T-shirt in the video for 'Where Are We Now?' or be aware that Hermione Farthingale acted in a movie called *Song of Norway* just after their relationship ended. We don't need to read 'The Bewlay Brothers' as a disguised exploration of David and Terry's relationship, or even know what 'Corinthian' means.

To me, for instance, 'comedian' and 'Corinthian' immediately conjure characters from Alan Moore's graphic novel *Watchmen* and Neil Gaiman's *Sandman*. My own personal associations are far from Bowie's intentions – his 'Uncle Arthur' is disparaged for being a Batman fan – but those comic book images of a costumed vigilante and a serial killer, respectively, seem tonally in tune with his moon boys and 'Kings of Oblivion', and they add my own mental pictures to his lyrics. As a teenager, I storyboarded short films in my head to 'Criminal World' and 'Cat People' without even seeing the videos, let alone knowing that 'Criminal World' was originally a 1977 track by Metro, or that there were two films called *Cat People*, from 1942 and 1982 (Bowie provided the soundtrack for the later one). I imagined vivid scenes from 'Ricochet' without doing any further research or reading, and over a decade before the internet. The images transfer from his crowded museum of a mental space to ours, filling it with, in Bakhtin's words, 'curious, odd, wondrous' items, 'adventures turned into things'. He shares them with us, and we make our own meanings from them.

Bowie's work doesn't need further research. We can simply enjoy the ideas he gifts us through his songs, without knowing where they come from, or what they originally meant. But following up his leads – and again, following his example, because he was a keen and impatient reader, an amateur film scholar, a broad-minded music fan, a respected art collector, and a devourer of visual culture – can make the experience richer.

Perhaps surprisingly, we can find examples of this approach applied even to Bowie's first LP, the collection of short stories and oddities from 1967. Of course, Anthony Newley is the first lead. We saw that the young David was inspired by *Stop the World – I Want to Get Off*, and he adjusts his own Bromley accent into an archly theatrical delivery for songs like 'Rubber Band' and 'Uncle Arthur'. 'I wanted to sing about things that directly influenced me at the time,' Bowie explained. 'Anthony Newley was the only singer who didn't put on a false American accent.' Paolo Hewitt's *Bowie: Album by Album* adds to this list of vocal influences, detecting traces of Pink Floyd's Syd Barrett and The Kinks' Ray Davies on 'There Is a Happy Land', 'and echoes of Burt Bacharach elsewhere'. Chris O'Leary, in turn, hears Judy Garland in the finale of 'The London Boys'.

Hewitt finds an origin for the counterpoint melodies of 'Sell Me a Coat' in Danny Kaye's 'Inchworm', from the 1952 film *Hans Christian Andersen*. O'Leary identifies another inspiration for 'Sell Me a Coat' in the Victorian children's books of Randolph Caldecott, and suggests a source for 'There Is a Happy Land' in Keith Waterhouse's novel of the same name.

He contextualises 'We Are Hungry Men' as Bowie's entry into the crowded field of 1960s science fiction and political dystopias such as *Quatermass*, *Doctor Who*, *The Day of the Triffids* and *The Population Bomb*. Nicholas Pegg suggests likely inspirations for 'The Laughing Gnome' in the jazz standard 'Little Brown Jug' and a 1952 novelty song, 'Pepino the Italian Mouse'.

Does it matter whether we know Bowie read these books, watched these films and listened to these songs? In some cases, the connection is secure: we can be sure that Bowie admired Newley in the 1960s, and that he admitted a debt to Danny Kaye's 'Inchworm'. ('You wouldn't believe the amount of my songs that have sort of spun off that one song,' he later explained, though he cited the nursery rhyme chorus of 'Ashes to Ashes' as the prime example.) We also know from interviews that he watched *The Quatermass Experiment* as a boy – from behind the sofa, when his parents thought he'd gone to bed – and that he named Keith Waterhouse as one of his favourite authors during the Deram period. Already, these links give us new avenues to explore, and we could spend days just following them up: watching *Quatermass* and *Hans Christian Andersen*, reading Waterhouse, listening to Anthony Newley. There's a reason why Bowie's Book Club caught on in 2018, encouraging fans to work their way through his recommended list of one hundred titles; and it isn't just because it's led by Duncan Jones. (Waterhouse's

Billy Liar is on there, but not the lesser-known *There Is a Happy Land*.)

By recreating Bowie's 1960s cultural experiences, we can broaden our own. During my year of immersive research, I trawled biographies for lists of his favourite films, novels and albums, and let myself be shaped by his tastes, shutting out the present day whenever possible. My pilgrimage was geographical and international – I read Evelyn Waugh's *Vile Bodies* at Los Angeles Airport, and listened to the O'Jays album *Back Stabbers* while walking the streets of Philadelphia – but I also gained an insight into his world while sitting at home in London watching the films he loved, from the obvious (*A Clockwork Orange* and *2001: A Space Odyssey*) to the more obscure (the 1957 drama *No Down Payment*, and Polanski's *A Knife in the Water*).

Some critical approaches would recommend that we stop there, with these solid leads, and insist that an echo of another work is only significant if we can be sure the author intended it. Others are less constrained in their interpretations and open up further possibilities.

Peter and Leni Gillman, for instance, sense 'the grip of his family mythology' throughout Bowie's 1967 debut album, and identify 'quite uncanny' echoes of his grandmother's poems in 'When I Live My Dream' and 'Sell Me a Coat'. They admit that Bowie probably never read these verses, but that does not dissuade them. They suggest instead that he was informed by a 'collective unconscious', and that 'David . . . drew from a creative fount whose precise nature and location remained a mystery even to him.' Their perspective is supported by his own admission that 'all I try to do in my writing is assemble points that interest me and puzzle through it, and that becomes a song.' He later went further: 'I'm the last one to understand most of the material I write.'

My own view is that while the detective work involved in discovering a firm influence is both fascinating and rewarding, it isn't the only way of interpreting Bowie. If I'd stuck to that rule, I would never have let my mind expand with the possibilities of 'Ricochet' – I would have only felt free to imagine what he intended, which in 1983 would have severely limited my choices. Researching the sources that shaped Bowie is part of the enjoyment, but it's also through our personal engagement with the songs that meaning emerges; our interpretation creates a framework from the fragments, and firms up their possibilities. Our interpretations can go beyond Bowie's original intentions. These aren't competitive quizzes, where the only point is to find out what he meant, and score top marks through solid answers; they are maps, where we can wander (and wonder) alone, or examine the signposts and see where they take us.

In the scholarly study of authorship, this approach is associated with post-structuralism, which identifies patterns, repeated themes and motifs across the work of an artist (a novelist, a film director, a folk singer), whether or not they are aware of them. Rather than seek out the author's intentions, post-structuralism places the responsibility for making meaning with the reader. If a song like 'Life on Mars?' depicts a dreamscape, we become interpreters of Bowie's unconscious, finding connections he may not have recognised himself. This theory emerged, coincidentally, at the same time as Bowie's first album: the key essay is Roland Barthes's 'The Death of the Author' from 1967. The title was deliberately provocative, and so was his argument. 'We know now,' Barthes wrote:

> that a text is not a line of words releasing a single 'theological' meaning (the 'message' of the Author-God) but a multidimensional space in which a variety of writings, none of them original, blend and clash. The text is a tissue of quotations drawn from the innumerable centres of culture... the writer can only imitate a gesture that is always anterior, never original.

As with Bowie, we don't need to look up every word to understand Barthes's key points. Rather than deferring to the author as a god-like authority, he suggests, we should see the text – a novel, a poem, a song lyric – as a multidimensional space (like a matrix) that draws on a multitude of other sources. If a Bowie song is a 'text', then the network of other writing it draws from is 'intertextual': we can think of it like a single station in relation to a map of the whole railway network, with each point joining up and connecting to others.

Originality, Barthes tells us, is impossible. Everything has been done before. So in that case, can artistic creativity really exist? Yes, according to Barthes, but not in the traditional sense of creating something from scratch. The author's 'only power is to mix writings, to counter the ones with the others, in such a way as never to rest on any one of them. Did he wish to *express himself*, he ought at least to know that the inner "thing" he thinks to "translate" is itself only a ready-formed dictionary, its words only explainable through other words, and so on indefinitely.'

The author, says Barthes, is limited to arranging existing phrases that have already been used by other writers. They should accept that every word is drawn from that network of existing material, and that their work can only make sense with reference to those other sources. Again, Barthes is taking an extreme position here, and deliberately countering the trend for seeing the author's intention as the guarantee of all meaning. He concludes that 'a text's unity lies not in its origin but its destination': not in the writer, but in us, the audience: 'a text is made of multiple writings, drawn from many cultures and entering into mutual relations of dialogue, parody, contestation, but there is one place where this multiplicity is focused and that place is the reader, not . . . the author.'

We can already see examples of how Barthes's theory might

work, by looking back at the examples above. Peter and Leni Gillman argued that Bowie's meanings 'remained a mystery even to him'. They saw their interpretation as valid, even without evidence, because Bowie had humbly absolved himself of the 'Author-God' role, placing authority in the reader instead: 'I'm the last one to understand most of the material I write.' As he said, 'all I try to do in my writing is assemble points that interest me' – which sounds very much like Barthes's account of an author drawing on pre-existing ideas, accepting that they can never be fully original, and arranging them into his own shapes and structures. Bowie's occasional reliance on cut-up techniques (whether physical or digital) and improvisation also suits the idea of song-writing as a kind of assembly, rather than the composition of an authoritative message from on high. In place of the traditional author, Barthes proposes the figure of the 'scriptor', who contains an 'immense dictionary from which he draws a writing that can know no halt'. Think of Bowie's impatient appetite for culture, and the way he poured out his scattered impressions into album after album, snatching quotations from novels, TV shows, movies and other songs: the description seems to fit him.

What about Barthes's idea that all writing is just 'a ready-formed dictionary, its words only explainable through other words, and so on indefinitely'? Looking more closely at another Bowie song provides a useful explanation.

'The Man Who Sold the World' (originally 1970) offers a particularly rich set of cross-references, even in its title alone. Paolo Hewitt states confidently that it was inspired by the 1950 Robert Heinlein novella *The Man Who Sold the Moon*. Chris O'Leary, describing it as a song with 'a score of absent fathers', suggests another science-fiction inspiration in Ray Bradbury's short story 'Night Meeting' (1950) where a man crosses paths with a Martian. Peter Doggett, whose book on Bowie is called *The Man Who Sold the World*, sees its precursors in a 1954 DC comic book, *The Man Who Sold the Earth*, and the 1968 Brazilian political satire *The Man Who Bought the World*.

Peter and Leni Gillman's biography links the lyric both to Wilfred Owen's 1919 poem 'Strange Meeting' and to a children's nursery rhyme ('Yesterday upon the stair, I met a man who wasn't there'). Chris O'Leary is more specific, sourcing the lines to 'The Little Man Who Wasn't There', a 1939 recording by the Glenn Miller Orchestra, and pointing out that this song, in turn, was adapted from William Hughes Mearns's longer poem 'Antagonish' from 1899.

The song seems to speak forward in time as well as backwards: to Bowie's 1976 film, *The Man Who Fell to Earth* (and the 1963 novel that inspired it) and to his threatening promise in 1983's 'China Girl' that 'I'll give you the man who wants to rule the world'. In 1993 a new generation saw Kurt Cobain cover the track on MTV's *Unplugged*, and assumed it was a

Nirvana song: others might remember it as a top ten hit for Lulu in 1974.

These diverse connections help us understand the concept of a Bowie song as 'a multi-dimensional space in which a variety of meanings, none of them original, blend and clash . . . a tissue of quotations drawn from the innumerable centres of culture'. None of these suggested sources match Bowie's explanation of his own motives, and that doesn't have to matter. For him, the song simply 'exemplified kind of how you feel when you're young . . . you have this great searching, this great need to find out who you really are'. Authorial intention is only part of the picture, and as Bowie wrote the song on the last day of mixing the album, its details are far more likely to have emerged from his unconscious than from deliberate research and referencing.

These interpretations, taken together, seem to give us a full sense of the matrix surrounding 'The Man Who Sold the World'. But we can follow the leads further. Bowie's song, we learned, echoes the Glenn Miller track, 'The Little Man Who Wasn't There', which was adapted from 'Antagonish', a verse by Hughes Mearns. Hughes Mearns's poem was, in turn, part of his play, *The Psycho-ed*. He'd been inspired by reports of a haunted house in a place called Antagonish. Where would we stop with this process of unpacking? What is Antagonish? A place in Nova Scotia. Who is Hughes Mearns? What is the Glenn Miller Orchestra? Who was Kurt

Cobain? What was Nirvana? There is no end to the avenues we could pursue from this single Bowie track. Every time we seem to reach a final explanation, it depends on the next one, 'its words only explainable through other words, and so on indefinitely'. This example adds another level of understanding to Barthes's phrase, 'a writing that can know no halt' and his assertion that meaning is 'infinitely deferred'. As post-structuralist philosophers Gilles Deleuze and Félix Guattari put it, 'every sign refers to another sign, and only to another sign, ad infinitum.' (And Bowie referred to them indirectly, too: his 1995 title 'A Small Plot of Land' paraphrases a line from their book, *A Thousand Plateaus*.) 'All signs are signs of signs. The question is not yet what a given sign signifies but to which other signs it refers, or which signs add themselves to it to form a network without beginning or end.'

This might make any interpretation of Bowie's lyrics seem an impossible task. If, entering the textual matrix of his work, we find ourselves pursuing endless avenues, where every reference leads to the next reference and every sign simply points us to another sign, in a 'network without beginning or end', is there any point in even starting?

The answer is that we choose how to create patterns from Bowie's work: where to start, and where to stop. It is our process of selection that makes sense of that 'fructile chaos' of fragments, and constructs meaning from it. We are not necessarily trying to discover a truth, because, as we've seen, the truth about Bowie and his lyrics is very hard to fix. We are creating a meaning in collaboration with him and the texts he left us. We are, in a way, answering the invitations he's given us since his earliest days of fame. 'I had to phone someone, so I picked on you' – with the famous finger-point at the *Top of the Pops* camera – from 'Starman'. 'Give me your hands, cause you're wonderful', from 'Rock 'n' Roll Suicide'. 'We could be heroes' was an anthem not for himself, but for all of us. Even among his last words, on *Blackstar* (also styled as the symbol, ★), there's a generous request for us to carry the torch for him: 'Spirit rose a metre and then stepped aside; somebody else took his place, and bravely cried.' By entering that complex network and picking out our own meaning, joining the dots of those scattered stars into our own pictures, we are Bowie's companions and co-authors, even now.

As we saw, it's possible to find echoes, intended or otherwise, between one theory and another, and join the dots across decades and disciplines. Fredric Jameson's description of postmodern art – 'in a world in which stylistic innovation is no longer possible, all that is left is to imitate dead styles, to speak through the masks and with the voices of the styles in the imaginary museum' – fits Bowie perfectly, with his costume changes, cast of characters, and literal, liberal use of make-up and masks, but it also dovetails with Barthes's proposal that nothing can be original, and that a work of art is a creative assembly of things that have been said before by other people: a 'multidimensional space', like a warehouse or museum. But while Barthes saw this idea as a liberation from traditional ideas of authorship, Jameson is more pessimistic.

'The writers and artists of the present day,' he warns, 'will no longer be able to invent new styles and worlds – they've already been invented; only a limited number of combinations are possible; the unique ones have been thought of already.' He sees this 'art about art' as a 'failure of the new, the imprisonment in the past', a redundant circuit of recycling which superficially quotes from previous work, without innovation or originality. Jameson fears that this plundering of the past will lead to the 'failure of art'.

Could this accusation be levelled at Bowie? As we saw, his first single, 'Liza Jane' was described as 'doubly derivative', while 'Louie, Louie Go Home' attempts a Lennon twang against Beatles-style harmonies. 'You've Got a Habit of Leaving' tended towards a Who sound, with Bowie approximating Roger Daltrey's vocals, while the B-side, 'Baby Loves That Way', copies both Herman's Hermits and The Kinks. Many of the songs on his debut album, of course, openly adopt Anthony Newley's style; some literally return to the past (the 1910s, in 'Rubber Band', and the Second World War in 'She's Got Medals') and others ('We Are Hungry Men',

'Please Mr Gravedigger') include snatches of fake news broadcasts, foreign accents and pantomime performances, as if
Bowie were dipping gleefully into a dressing-up box.

His first hit, 'Space Oddity', borrows from Simon and
Garfunkel's 'Old Friends' for its 'sitting in a tin can' section;
the vocal on 'Janine', from the 1969 LP, is a committed
impression of Elvis Presley, complete with growls and whoops.
On 1971's *Hunky Dory*, Bowie pulls off a convincing Bob
Dylan impersonation, and offers an entire song, 'Queen Bitch',
in the style of Lou Reed and the Velvet Underground. By the
time he released *Pin Ups*, his album of covers from 1973, he'd
already racked up an LP's worth of tribute numbers in various
forms: and this was two years before he started borrowing
from the soul catalogue with *Young Americans*.

During his subsequent career, we could argue, he recycles
not just broad themes (time, fame, death, madness) but specific
motifs from his own earlier work. 'Ashes to Ashes' unashamedly begins with a nostalgic call-back to 'Space Oddity' – 'do
you remember a guy that's been / in such an early song' – and
both 1995's 'Hallo Spaceboy' and 'Blackstar', from his final
album, have been interpreted as further episodes in the Major
Tom saga. 'Buddha of Suburbia' (1993) recycles the strummed
guitar and handclaps from 'Space Oddity', and ends with a
chorus of *'zane zane zane, ouvre le chien'*, lifted from 1970's 'All
the Madmen'. 'You Feel So Lonely You Could Die', from 2013,
adapts the drum pattern from 'Five Years', forty-one years

earlier. 'Everyone Says Hi' (2002) incorporates the '*bap-bap-ba-whoo*' backing vocals from 'Absolute Beginners' (1986). The cover art for *Scary Monsters* reworks images from *Low*, '*Heroes*' and *Lodger*; while *The Next Day* draws on '*Heroes*' again, covering the earlier photo with a plain white square and crossing out the title. We could certainly find evidence to show that Bowie is stuck in a postmodern short-circuit, copying other people's styles and then raiding his own storehouse for ideas.

However, it doesn't take much further examination to undermine this argument. Bowie's modification of the '*Heroes*' image, far from lazy recycling, has a profound, even philosophical significance, which we'll explore further in the final chapter. His nods back to earlier songs add up to a handful of quotations, scattered across fifty years of original work: the reference to Major Tom in 'Hallo Spaceboy' only occurs in the Pet Shop Boys remix, and 'Blackstar' simply features a mysterious jewelled space helmet, open to interpretation. As for his pastiche of other artists' vocal style, what starts off as impressions – trying on someone else's persona for size, as a front to hide behind – becomes more complex as Bowie gains confidence. 'Janine' might sound superficially like an Elvis track, but the lyrics and themes are pure Bowie, from the line 'I've got to keep my veil on my face' to the axe that threatens to kill 'another man, not me at all', and of course that 'strange demand to collocate my mind'.

We can say the same for the other examples. 'Song for Bob Dylan' is drawled with Dylan's intonation, but it also comments on that 'voice like sand and glue'; it's both a song that Dylan might have written, and a song about him, from the perspective of a critical fan. In a further layer of self-conscious referentiality, Bowie's title recalls Dylan's own 'Song to Woody', from 1962. It may be art about art, but it's fully aware of its own part in the process. 'Queen Bitch', similarly, is a tribute to the Velvets that approximates Lou Reed's hard-boiled spoken delivery, but filters it through Bowie's experience and perspective. 'Satin and tat' is a disparaging phrase borrowed from his mime tutor, Lindsay Kemp – a line from backstage at British theatres, rather than Harlem bars – and the basic riff is Eddie Cochran's 'Three Steps to Heaven', a throwback to the American rock that formed the backdrop to Bowie's teenage years.

While the lyrics convincingly and casually mention characters like 'Sister Flo' – a possible cousin of the Velvets' 'Sister Ray' – Bowie's character is 'up on the eleventh floor, watching the cruisers below'. He's a spectator to the street-level cast, staying in his solitary hotel room and gazing at the wall, declaring bitterly that the guy downstairs 'could have been me'.

This jaded outsider is a distinctly Bowie protagonist of the period. The final verse of 'Panic in Detroit' (1973) finds the narrator in a similar position, as he escapes the chaos outside and races back to his room; the song concludes with him gazing out of the window as he did in 'Queen Bitch', searching the sky for planes and wishing someone would phone. Again, there's a charismatic mover and shaker at the centre of the action (here, he 'looked a lot like Che Guevara'), but it's not Bowie himself. 'Watch That Man', from the same year, is also narrated by a fascinated outsider: here, Bowie takes the role of a gossip correspondent reporting on the party scene, torn between wariness and frank admiration for the social master-mind who's pulling everyone's strings. 'He walks like a jerk but he's only taking care of the room.'

Though 'Queen Bitch' sounds like a Velvets track, then, its attitude anticipates *Aladdin Sane* and the nervous, outsider energy of 'Ziggy in America', which is quite different from Lou Reed's take on the urban environments he knows well. Reed's 'Walk on the Wild Side', to use an obvious example from 1972, takes us at a leisurely, relaxed pace through a series of short stories, introducing us to the locals and talking through their history – here's Holly, Candy, Little Joe and Jackie, and here's how they got here. 'Sweet Jane', 'Candy Says', 'Femme Fatale' and 'All Tomorrow's Parties' share that lingering, unhurried approach to character. Reed and the Velvets are insiders who know the scene and its people.

Bowie's 'Watch That Man', by contrast, races frantically through fragmented glimpses of a social whirl, rushing us past Shakey, Lorraine and the Reverend Alabaster without any context or explanation. America is a blitz of impressions, and Bowie observes it like a fascinated tourist peering through the windows of his tour car – as he did in the 1975 documentary *Cracked Actor* – or even more dispassionately, as if he's watching scenes projected on a hotel wall. He can name-check with the best of them, but he remains alienated rather than an insider, watching another man. 'Queen Bitch' is a Velvet Underground song that's been through the Bowie matrix; it incorporates aspects of Lou Reed's style and milieu, but is at least equally shaped by Bowie's experiences in the 1960s, and his preoccupations of the early 1970s.

We can see the way Bowie dips into that museum (or storehouse, or warehouse) and draws existing ideas into his own creative framework by looking more closely at the *Diamond Dogs* LP of 1974. Like Bowie's other attempts at a concept album (such as *Ziggy Stardust* and the later *1. Outside*), *Diamond Dogs* quickly gives up on narrative, and offers a compilation of songs vaguely based around the theme of gleeful, glam apocalypse. It has its origins in various bold projects that went awry, reached a dead-end, changed their form and were welded together; it's a composite, a compromise.

In November 1973 he'd met the novelist William Burroughs, who sparked his interest in 'cut-up' techniques where a text was sliced to pieces, then rearranged into a new, surprising composition. He marvelled at the 'wonder-house of strange shapes and colours, tastes, feelings' it created. Also crowding up his mental warehouse (or wonder-house) at the time were plans for a Ziggy Stardust musical ('forty scenes are in it,' he blithely declared, suggesting it would be 'nice' if the actors shuffled them about into a new order for each performance), another musical called *Tragic Moments*, and an album called *Revenge, or The Best Haircut I Ever Had*. And if that wasn't enough, he casually dropped another plan: 'I'm doing Orwell's *Nineteen Eighty-Four* on television.'

He wasn't. George Orwell's widow, Sonia, refused to grant permission: she'd given a licence for earlier, more sober and faithful adaptations, and regretted those. 'Do you think I'm turning *this* over to *that* as a musical?' she asked him scathingly – according to Bowie, who of course is not always a reliable source. Many of his offhand boasts at the time are either provocations or experiments; in some cases he may have genuinely wanted to hear how an idea sounded when it was spoken out loud. He did not, of course, release *Tragic Moments*, either, or *The Best Haircut I Ever Had*, or the protest songs he was planning about 'how bad the food in Harrods is these days,' which would have been – if they ever existed – a smugly ironic inversion of his social realist shoplifting song, 'God Knows I'm Good', from 1969. *Diamond Dogs* is a compromise, but it is a happier compromise than some of the possible alternatives.

The final album includes songs from the mooted Ziggy musical ('Rebel Rebel' and 'Rock 'n' Roll with Me') which was dumped because Bowie decided, sensibly, that it would be a dated step backwards. These are combined with remnants of the *Nineteen Eighty-Four* project (a trilogy on the B-side, comprising 'We Are the Dead', '1984', and 'Big Brother') and headed up with tracks inspired more by Burroughs and Dickens than Orwell. 'It still implied the idea of the breakdown of a city,' Bowie explained, 'a disaffected youth that no longer had home-unit situations, but lived as gangs on roofs and really had the city to themselves.' That metropolis was named 'Hunger City' in the introductory track, 'Future Legend', and described vividly in 'Diamond Dogs' itself, where Hallowe'en Jack 'lives on top of Manhattan Chase' and slides down to the streets on a rope like Tarzan. Bowie claimed to be equally inspired by Burroughs' 1971 novel *The Wild Boys*, Dickens' *Oliver Twist* – 'what if Fagin's gang had gone absolutely ape-shit?' – and by his father's stories of Dr Barnardo finding urchin scavengers on the parapets of London buildings. Already, then, *Nineteen Eighty-Four* was meshed and merged (as we'd now say, mashed-up) with a wide range of other texts; it was just one influencing factor alongside Victorian literature, Beat prose-poetry, social history (filtered through family), and the myth of Ziggy Stardust. They all fed into Bowie's consciousness and were spat out through a cut-up process that fragmented them still further.

This may sound a long way from a musical version of Orwell's novel, and of course in a way it is; but it is also not so different to the way any adaptation works. Contemporary critical theory has moved on from the idea that a novel must be translated faithfully to another medium; indeed, it claims that this kind of straight translation is impossible. Instead, it draws on ideas of an intertextual matrix exactly like the ones we've considered already, and uses the same post-structuralist theory.

Robert Stam proposes, for instance, that adaptation is not translation, but 'reaccentuation, whereby a source work is reinterpreted through new grids and discourses'. Instead of a straightforward pairing between the source text and the new version for a different medium, he sees 'an open structure, constantly reworked and reinterpreted by a boundless context', within which 'the text feeds on and is fed into an infinitely permutating intertext, seen through ever-shifting grids of interpretation.'

These are complex ideas, but we have encountered them before, in only slightly different terms. An ever-shifting grid is a network or a matrix, or in Barthes's phrase, 'a multidimensional space in which a variety of writings, none of them original, blend and clash'. Barthes envisioned 'a writing that can know no halt', a process where meaning is 'infinitely deferred'. Gilles Deleuze and Félix Guattari suggested that 'every sign refers to another sign, and only to another sign, ad infinitum,' in 'a network without beginning or end'. We saw how this could work through the example of 'The Man Who Sold the World' and its multiple sources, which lead us back endlessly through further references.

Mikhail Bakhtin, the theorist who described literature as a metaphorical castle full of curious objects, also proposed that all meaning in a text (a book, a musical, a song) was created through a dialogue between its author, its readers and the other texts that it inevitably brushes up against. Sonia Orwell wanted to protect *Nineteen Eighty-Four* and keep its integrity intact, but while she succeeded on a legal level, it's conceptually impossible to seal any published work off from other influences. The novel had already been interpreted differently by each of its readers, and currently operates in its own intertextual matrix where '1984' is not just a Bowie track or a series of film adaptations but also an increasingly distant year in history; where 'Big Brother' is not just a concept in her husband's book, but a Bowie song and, more famously, the name of a reality show. Rather than compromising and corrupting the original, Bakhtin would suggest that the novel 'lives and takes shape' through this fluid process, rather than existing in static isolation. *Diamond Dogs* has undergone the same process: it is now also the title of a 2017 *Doctor Who* novel, a military squad in the *Metal Gear Solid* video games, a brand of hot dog stands, and a company selling luxury collars for 'people and their pets'.

Orwell's *Nineteen Eighty-Four* was, if we agree with Barthes, already a compilation from various sources, a creatively arranged composition of pre-existing ideas: Orwell, of course, drew on his own influences such as his experiences of the

BBC, his understanding of the USSR under Stalin, Huxley's *Brave New World*, and the work of H. G. Wells. Now it circulates in a broader, mobile, never-ending network of meanings that increases every year: his notion of 'doublethink' has, for instance, acquired a new use during the Trump administration. As philosopher Julia Kristeva suggests, 'any text is constructed as a mosaic of quotations; any text is the absorption and transformation of another.' Every text is already an adaptation, and every adaptation will, in turn, incorporate other influences, depending in part on the cultural moment when it is made. To choose a classic example, the *Henry V* starring Laurence Olivier, part-funded by the British government as the Second World War drew to a close in 1944, is based on exactly the same play as Kenneth Branagh's post-Falklands (and post-Vietnam) *Henry V* of 1989, but the depiction of military conflict in the two films is dramatically different.

Orwell's novel circulates under the same conditions. The 1956 production of *1984* substitutes 'Calidor' for the traitor Goldstein, avoiding any negative, post-war associations with a Jewish name. The 1984 adaptation, directed by Michael Radford, was shot on the precise dates and in the locations mentioned in the novel, and takes place against London backdrops, like Battersea Power Station, that have since been radically transformed. The 1953 BBC play *Nineteen Eighty-Four*, starring Peter Cushing, has Winston Smith living and working in what would then have been a modern, even 'futuristic' environment, with clean, sterile lines, plastic decor and slick automation; the 1984 production is, by contrast, set in a grimy, retro-1940s city. The next movie adaptation of *Nineteen Eighty-Four* will surely, in turn, be informed by the more recent concepts of fake news and post-truth.

Bowie's take on *Nineteen Eighty-Four* certainly occupies the looser end of the adaptation spectrum, but its free, fluid borrowing of themes, motifs and key dialogue is not without precedent: Peter Greenaway steers Shakespeare's *The Tempest* towards his own aesthetic style and interests in *Prospero's Books* (1991), and the chick-flick comedies *Bridget Jones's Diary* (2001) and *Clueless* (1995) play fast and loose with Austen's *Pride and Prejudice* and *Emma* respectively. 'The diamond dogs are poachers,' Bowie explains in the title track; it also describes his own approach, a selective pilfering.

The Eurythmics soundtrack LP for the 1984 film, *1984: For the Love of Big Brother*, offers an interesting contrast to *Diamond Dogs*. While it devotes a whole album, rather than just three songs, to the novel's themes – and lifts passages of Newspeak directly from the page – director Michael Radford objected to its synthesised electronica, and preferred the plainer, orchestral score he'd intended. Bowie's homage to *Nineteen Eighty-Four* is idiosyncratic, certainly, but even a more straightforward tribute to Orwell's work can never be entirely 'faithful'. (The Eurythmics did, unlike Bowie, go on to release an album called *Revenge*.)

What, then, does *Diamond Dogs* adapt from the original text? Though the title of the introductory track, 'Future Legend', fits Orwell's project – and its Temperance Building, with slowly lifting shutters, could double for the Ministry of Love – its lurid descriptions of dystopia owe more to other authors. Nicholas Pegg sees the influence of William Burroughs in the 'ten thousand peoploids split into small tribes coveting the highest of the sterile skyscrapers, like packs of dogs', and David Buckley agrees that the line paraphrases *The Naked Lunch* with its 'baying pack of people'. Chris O'Leary identifies another possible source in Ray Bradbury's *Something Wicked This Way Comes*: Bowie gleefully tells us that 'fleas the size of rats sucked on rats the size of cats', while Bradbury's 1962 novel includes 'rats which fed on spiders which fed, in turn, because they were large enough, on cats.' Rats, as Pegg points out, play a key role in *Nineteen Eighty-Four*, as Winston Smith's greatest fear, and may have crept into Bowie's warehouse of influences for this track, which falls outside the more obvious suite of three Orwell songs.

Even in those three songs however, critics have to search hard for any traces of the novel, beyond the obvious titles. Nicholas Pegg and Chris O'Leary note the echo of Thought Police boots in Bowie's 'I hear them on the stairs' from 'We Are the Dead' (Orwell describes 'a stampede of boots up the stairs' when Winston is discovered with his lover Julia). Peter Doggett ambitiously reads 'the stunted humanity of Winston's life, from his first encounter with Julia to his vain hope of marking their union with a child', into lines like 'I looked at you and wondered if you saw things my way.' The lyrics 'it's a twenty-four-hour service, guaranteed to make you tell,' seem a likely reference to the interrogation Winston faces in the Ministry of Love and Room 101.

While there are multiple references to a powerful leader in 'Big Brother' ('Someone to claim us, someone to follow'), along with descriptions that could readily match the novel's surveillance society ('we'll build a glass asylum') and its Junior Anti-Sex League ('we'll be living from sin'), O'Leary looks beyond literal meaning and searches instead for metaphorical parallels in the song's arrangement. 'A baritone saxophone prods you along like a warder . . . are there any signs of resistance? Bowie's 12-string acoustic guitar, running underground for much of the track?' Similarly, Doggett hears 'Winston's tentative belief in Julia' through the studio processing of Bowie's voice, 'heavily echoed throughout the verse, almost half a beat behind', on 'We Are the Dead'.

O'Leary's take on the title track of Bowie's never-made musical, in turn, focuses more on 1973 than 1984, and revisits the 'grey paralyzed Britain' that Bowie was about to leave as he relocated to the US for tax purposes: an 'anemic reenactment of the war years . . . there was government-mandated rationing . . . there were bombs going off in London . . . there were some fascist ramblings in the establishment.'

Nicholas Pegg barely mentions Orwell in his account of the song; instead, he tracks its origins as the opening number from the NBC TV special, *The 1980 Floor Show* (1973) – another typically corny Bowie pun – where it was merged with the lesser-known 'Dodo'.

Not included on *Diamond Dogs*, and relegated to Bowie's back catalogue, 'Dodo' also incorporates aspects of Orwell's novel, in a fractured, scattered form: as such, it expands Bowie's *Nineteen Eighty-Four* songs to a more substantial suite of four musical numbers – or five, if we also include 'Chant of the Ever Circling Skeletal Family', which segues smoothly from 'Big Brother' and concludes the album. With its repeated syllable 'bruh, bruh, bruh', it seems to be Bowie's version of the 'Two Minutes Hate' from *Nineteen Eighty-Four*: in Orwell's description, 'the entire group of people broke into a slow, rhythmical chant of "B-B! B-B!".' 'Dodo' also incorporates a dumb, monosyllabic repetition in its chorus: 'he's a do-do . . . no, no . . . didn't hear it from me', with a hint of *Nineteen Eighty-Four*'s 'duckspeak', the term for mindlessly repeating political orthodoxies.

'Dodo' further confirms that Orwell's novel was firmly installed in Bowie's mental framework at the time, though the references are, again, gestures towards the source text rather than precise quotations. 'Now we can talk in confidence,' the live version begins, echoing covert conversations about the resistance between Winston, Julia and O'Brien.

'You know that we've been done wrong.' The second verse revisits scenes from *Nineteen Eighty-Four* where the party-faithful children of Winston's neighbour, Parsons, observe and then inform on him for supposed thoughtcrime. 'It was almost normal for people over thirty to be frightened of their own children,' Winston reflects. 'And with good reason, for hardly a week passed in which *The Times* did not carry a photograph describing how some eavesdropping little sneak – "child hero" was the phrase generally used – had overheard some compromising remark and denounced its parents to the Thought Police.' Bowie had already touched on the idea in 'We Are the Dead', with 'we're breaking in the new boys, deceive your next of kin.'

In 'Dodo', a citizen 'thinks he's well-screened from the man at the top' – itself a possible pun on Big Brother's ever-present telescreens – but 'it's a shame that his children disagree.' They 'coolly decide to sell him down the line', Bowie declares. 'Daddy's brainwashing time.' A later verse continues the theme: it describes waking up under a scorching light, to find that 'neighbour Jim' has come to turn you in. 'Jim' is Bowie's invention – all Winston's friends refer to each other by surnames – but the constant risk of exposure is entirely true to the novel. 'Didn't hear it from me', the song's alternative title, reinforces the paranoia. Rather than attempting a straight adaptation of events, Bowie inserts himself within the novel's dystopian environment, and creates a side narrative for its minor characters: we might call it fan fiction, a collaboration between the two writers.

Is this the full extent of Bowie's engagement with *Nineteen Eighty-Four*? As we saw, Pegg and O'Leary, who both devote entire books to a detailed study of each song in turn, find few obvious connections in '1984' itself, and foreground other aspects like the song's production and social context. It's worth looking closely again at that title track, though, because its engagement with Orwell's novel is more extensive and subtle than they suggest. This song in particular leads us to a fuller understanding not just of how Bowie engages with this particular text, but how he adapts in general: how he incorporates, quotes, modifies and combines from a range of diverse sources, forming them into his own distinct arrangement.

Bowie's most obvious borrowings in '1984', beyond the title, are single key words: his song's enforcers 'tell you that you're *eighty*, but *brother* you won't care'. It's as if he's cut up a summary of the novel and strewn it across his own page, seeing where the fragments stick and writing a new context around them. There's a more fundamental thematic echo in this line too, though, beyond the superficial. Winston's punishment and cure involve accepting what he's told in the name of Big Brother – even embracing the idea that $2 + 2$ can equal 5 – however ridiculous the numbers sound. During the process, O'Brien makes him face his own physical decay, and

Winston shuffles his skeletal body to the mirror, realising he looks much older than his actual age. 'At a guess he would have said that it was the body of a man of sixty.' (They'll 'tell you that you're eighty'.) As Bowie advises in the opening couplet, the prisoner's only option is compliance now, in the face of future destruction: 'Some day they won't let you, so now you must agree.' 'It might be a long time,' O'Brien muses. 'But . . . in the end we shall shoot you.'

The rest of the song is peppered with phrases and imagery reminiscent of the novel. 'The tracks are on TV' may bring telescreens to mind, while the plea 'remember me' recalls the loss of history and identity in *Nineteen Eighty-Four*, with its censored past and erased 'unpersons'. The chorus, 'beware the savage jaw of 1984', seems to reprise the threat of Winston's rats: 'they will leap on to your face and bore straight into it,' as O'Brien coldly explains. 'Tomorrow's never there,' meanwhile, evokes Winston's desperate, doomed attempts to envision a future beyond Big Brother. 'Somehow you will fail,' he tells O'Brien during the torture sessions. 'Something will defeat you. Life will defeat you.' O'Brien closes down his hopes: 'If you want a picture of the future, imagine a boot stamping on a human face – for ever.' After his re-education, Winston is 'much better', brainwashed into blandly supporting the state. 'Everything was all right, the struggle was finished,' the novel concludes. 'They'll split your pretty cranium,' Bowie warns at the start of his second verse, 'and fill it full of air.'

We could argue that Bowie's lyrics here are simply standard tropes of dystopian science fiction, which recur in similar forms through his other songs: the predictions of apocalypse in 'Five Years', the offhand pessimism that 'a plague seems quite feasible now' from 'Saviour Machine', the silver screens in 'Life on Mars?' and 'Andy Warhol'. The lyric 'we played an all-night movie role', from '1984', could nod back to the novel's tele-screen surveillance, or serve simply as another evocation of cinematic decadence, like the 'video films we saw' in the earlier 'Drive-In Saturday'. A line like 'the bodies on the screen stopped bleeding' could, in turn, fit easily into '1984' and be read as a reference to the novel's newsreels of war and atrocity: but it's a casual remark from 'Watch That Man'.

As Nicholas Pegg notes, 'they'll split your pretty cranium and fill it full of air' can also be seen as a rewrite of the line 'day after day, they take some brain away' from 'All the Madmen'; as such, it could be as much a reference to Terry Burns as to George Orwell. Indeed, Peter and Leni Gillman, whose biography is centred around Bowie's family relationships, even see 'Big Brother' as 'an appeal to his half-brother Terry', and 'Chant of the Ever Circling Skeletal Family' as a reminder of the Jones heritage. The coda to 'Big Brother' that concludes the album, which is heard by some listeners as 'bruh, bruh, bruh' and others as 'riot, riot, riot', provides a neat microcosm of Bowie's work as a whole: multiple meanings are equally available at the same time. Are we stretching the interpretation if we try to list every possible link between the song and the novel, forcing connections that may be accidental?

Certainly, Bowie was already preoccupied with technology, tyranny, social hierarchy and the end of days by the time he wrote *Diamond Dogs*. 'Saviour Machine', from 1970, offers his own fable of a leader called President Joe, whose invention 'stopped war, gave them food, how they adored'. His machine is nicknamed the Prayer, and the song's chorus raises a chant of 'please don't believe in me', a precursor of 'please, saviour, saviour, show us' from the later 'Big Brother'. 'The Man Who Sold the World' also describes a conversation with an enigmatic, powerful figure who 'said I was his friend' and 'never lost control', while its vision of millions who 'must have died alone, a long long time ago' chimes with 'We Are the Dead', the 'Ever Circling Skeletal Family' and, in the original novel, Winston's grim understanding that 'he was already dead' as soon as he commits thoughtcrime. The man who sold the world, we might remember, also 'passed upon the stair', like the Thought Police in 'We Are the Dead'.

Meanwhile, 'Oh! You Pretty Things' and 'Quicksand', from 1971's *Hunky Dory*, explore ideas of the 'homo superior', borrowed from Nietzsche and Aleister Crowley; in *Nineteen Eighty-Four*, an elite Inner Party dominates both the Outer Party and the proletariat, who are dismissed as mere animals. O'Brien taunts Winston: 'and you consider yourself morally

superior to us, with our lies and our cruelty? . . . You are the
last man.' All those tracks – 'Saviour Machine', 'The Man
Who Sold the World', 'Oh! You Pretty Things' and 'Quicksand'
– could feasibly be included in an imaginary musical of *Nineteen
Eighty-Four*.

Are the motifs, themes and tropes of '1984' just typical of
Bowie's early seventies work, then, or are they a series of
references to the novel? Yes, is the only answer: they're both.
Rather than a conventional adaptation, the songs left over
from Bowie's abandoned musical mark an intersection between
Bowie and Orwell's text, where his ideas merge with *Nineteen
Eighty-Four*. We can envisage them as two separate networks,
or matrices, which combine and overlap. Many elements of
Orwell's story are lost in the process, but the common aspects
are emphasised: the worship of leaders, the rise of superior
social castes, the fascination with mind-control, the seductive
risks of technology. To give a specific example, we don't have
to decide whether the line 'they'll split your pretty cranium
and fill it full of air' is about Winston Smith or Terry Burns.
As we saw in the previous chapter, two things can be true at
the same time. Orwell called it doublethink; we could see it
more positively as double vision, offering us the twinned
perspective of two textual maps, one from 1948 and one from
1973, laid over each other.

Nineteen Eighty-Four gave Bowie a set, props, characters
and costumes through which to explore the ideas he'd been

playing with for years; he brought his hedonistic glam excess to the grim squalor of Orwell's future London. Another line from '1984' provides a perfect example of how the process worked. The third verse begins, 'I'm looking for a party, I'm looking for a side.' Orwell's society is structured around the Party, but Bowie, of course, is also looking for a different kind of party, like the one Shakey threw in 'Watch That Man', where 'everybody drank a lot of something nice'. It's an easy pun, but it also works as a pivot between two levels: the social whirl typical of *Aladdin Sane* (and Bowie's own lifestyle) and the rigid political structures of the novel, and leads us to a more complex dynamic in the next line: 'I'm looking for the treason that I knew in '65.'

To Bowie, composing in 1973, the year 1984 was, of course, still in the future, as it had been for Orwell when he wrote the novel in 1948. Bowie, however, had lived through the 1960s and early 1970s, which to Orwell were almost as distant as 1984, and could only be imagined. This distinction may seem obvious, but it adds a further dimension to the doubled perspective between '1984' and *Nineteen Eighty-Four*: the inter-section between the matrix of the novel's world, and the network of distinct but overlapping ideas that Bowie brought to it. As O'Leary pointed out, the real-world social issues of 1973 shaped Bowie's approach, and in this context, 'looking for the treason that I knew in '65' reads like 'a dark Sixties retrospective'. O'Leary suggests, along the same lines, that

'Big Brother' represents 'a fragment of the past, the voice of some Arts Lab hippie about to be turned out on the street'.

He means Bowie's lived past, the 1960s that had actually taken place, and his interpretation interlocks with what we know of Bowie's end-of-decade disillusionment: 'Cygnet Committee' and 'Memory of a Free Festival' (both 1969) articulate his disappointment with and growing contempt for the folk scene. But there is an intriguing double meaning to the line. *Nineteen Eighty-Four* is not just about the future; it also has its own detailed internal history. In one passage, Winston remembers a key moment when 'just once in his life he had possessed . . . concrete, unmistakeable evidence of an act of falsification. He had held it between his fingers for as long as thirty seconds. In 1973, it must have been.' One of the most significant memories in Winston's life, then, overlaps with the year when Bowie was composing his songs; it must have felt uncanny to Bowie, reading that date and knowing that to Orwell, it was an imagined future. 'But the really relevant date,' Winston goes on, 'was seven or eight years earlier.'

Over the next paragraphs, Winston remembers the events of the middle sixties, when the original leaders of the revolution were wiped out. 'Among the last survivors were three men named Jones, Aaronson, and Rutherford. It must have been in 1965 that these three had been arrested . . . they had confessed to intelligence with the enemy . . . embezzlement of public funds, the murder of various trusted Party members.' Winston, holding out hope for another revolution, is 'looking for the treason that I knew in '65'. Bowie may well be remembering the end of the hippy movement during his own 1960s, but – unless we assume he read the novel carelessly, not picking up on this passage at all – he was looking back down parallel timelines, seeing his own matrix of experiences alongside the framework of Orwell's text. Not one or the other, but both.

Bowie's loose suite of five songs – '1984', 'We Are the Dead', 'Big Brother', the short 'Chant of the Ever Circling Skeletal Family' and, beyond the finished *Diamond Dogs* LP, 'Dodo' – does not add up to a conventional adaptation of *Nineteen Eighty-Four* by any means. In some ways, though, it offers more than that. He integrates his reading of the novel with his own experiences and his existing obsessions, throwing diverse cultural cross-references into the mix. Alongside its paraphrases of Orwell's ideas, '1984' includes a near-quotation from Bob Dylan – 'the times they are a-telling, and the changing isn't free' – and its introduction is lifted from Isaac Hayes's 'Theme From Shaft' (1971). 'Big Brother' opens with a no-nonsense dismissal of Bowie's previous album – 'don't talk of dust and roses' – turning its nose up at *Aladdin Sane*'s title track, with its airy, self-indulgent decadence. ('Watching him dash away,' that song begins, 'swinging an old bouquet – dead roses.') The turn towards funk, combined with Bowie's grand baritones, points towards the next LP, *Young Americans*.

The result is not *Nineteen Eighty-Four*, but a mosaic made of its smashed-up parts, scattered and stuck down again in new formations, alongside material from a future Orwell couldn't imagine.

If this cut-up technique, which resulted in lines like 'you're just an ally of the leecher, locator for the virgin king, but I love you in your fuck-me pumps' ('We Are the Dead'), seems a long way from Orwell's considered prose, the approach itself is in keeping with *Nineteen Eighty-Four*. As O'Brien says: 'Power is in tearing human minds to pieces and putting them together again in new shapes of your own choosing.' Other ideas from Orwell filter through into Bowie's later work: the proles of *Nineteen Eighty-Four* listen to songs 'composed without any human intervention whatever on an instrument known as a versificator'. Bowie's mid-1990s cut-ups were achieved using a Verbasizer. More fundamentally, his tendency to rewrite his own history is straight out of the Ministry of Truth's playbook.

Bowie returned to the novel's specific milieu in 1995's *1. Outside*, admitting in an interview that his character Algeria Touchshriek was 'very much' indebted to Charrington, the man who rents Winston a secret room above a second-hand shop. 'A very English character, he's almost the stereotypical shop owner,' Bowie enthused. Touchshriek, who deals in 'art drugs and DNA prints', is also 'thinking of leasing the room above my shop'. But most tellingly, Bowie merges the name of his character with Orwell's. 'Aha! Catshriek!' he exclaims to the interviewer, creating a mutant hybrid of the two. It's technically wrong, but fundamentally right. It captures perfectly the meshing of Bowie's mental warehouse with Orwell's world, where Charrington's shop stocks 'dusty picture-frames . . . trays of nuts and bolts, worn-out chisels, pen-knives with broken blades . . . lacquered snuff-boxes, agate brooches, and the like'. The tiny interior was, Orwell notes, 'uncomfortably full'. The metaphors crowd together, overlapping in an echo chamber. *My brain hurt like a warehouse, there was no room to spare.* An imaginary museum of masks, voices and costumes from the past. Literature as a space packed with 'isolated curiosities and rarities . . . self-sufficient items – curious, odd, wondrous . . . congealed "suddenlys", adventures turned into things'. The cut-up technique as a 'wonder-house of strange shapes and colours, tastes, feelings'. These are all the same ideas, criss-crossing through the multiple matrices of Bakhtin, Jameson, Orwell and Bowie.

Studying Bowie's approach to, and appropriation from, *Nineteen Eighty-Four* is important for what it reveals about his approach to culture as a whole. Rather than convert the novel to a new medium – his musical would never have worked, not least because he didn't have the patience to sustain a story over a concept album – he immersed himself in it, lifting items freely from its storehouse (or museum, or second-hand shop) and combining them with others from his own collection. This, rather than straight translation, superficial pastiche or lazy theft, was his *modus operandi* towards art. The materials he used may, in many cases, have been borrowed from others (though as we've learned, they were never fully original), but it was the way he combined and juxtaposed them that gave them his signature. We can learn a lot from his approach; it provides us with a guide for how to incorporate Bowie into our own lives.

It might well seem that I didn't practise what I'm preaching here. When I decided to immerse myself in Bowie's life for a year of my own, I was surely attempting more of a faithful adaptation, trying to transform myself into Bowie and translate his past experiences into mine. To an extent, that's true. I aimed at a certain level of authenticity, setting and sticking to rules where I could. As part of my attempt to recreate and immerse myself in his cultural headspace, for instance, I would never listen to music more recent than the 'current' year of my research. The make-up artists I hired brought only cosmetics that would have been available in the early 1970s: thicker creams and cakey powders. I could take that off at the end of the day, but I couldn't change my hair, which was dyed the copper and blond of Bowie's *Man Who Fell to Earth* period.

I held long consultations with a costume designer – whose other clients included the girl band Little Mix and the contestants on *Strictly Come Dancing* – about the exact shade of red for my duplicate of Bowie's dungarees from the 'Rebel Rebel' video.

We ended up cutting up and stitching together two vintage shirts to reproduce the pattern on his blouse as closely as possible. To record my experiences, I used analogue equipment: cameras from the 1970s and 1980s, and film stock so rare it could only be processed by hand by a specialist in Berlin.

Other aspects were harder to simulate. Reducing Bowie's mid-seventies isolation at his house on North Doheny Drive, Los Angeles, to a single, intense week, I booked a hotel room and stayed there with the curtains closed, restricting myself to his infamous diet of red peppers and milk, and reading Crowley and Nietzsche. I invited people to visit who weren't so much friends as acquaintances; people with fringe views and unpredictable moods. I was trying to feel my way into the persona of the Thin White Duke, Bowie's cruel and arrogant crooner: and the combination of solitude and strange company, along with the things I was putting in my body and feeding into my head, made it worryingly easy, even though I wasn't in 1970s LA, and didn't come close to killing myself with cocaine.

Like Bowie, I escaped to Berlin for a change of scene. At

the end of August 2015 I stored the early seventies outfits in my attic and brought down the clothes I'd bought in advance the previous month: the leather jacket and trenchcoat, the check shirt and flat cap. I had my hair cut and coloured into a brunette quiff, and did my best over the next two weeks to grow a convincing moustache. Bowie had tried to pass as anonymous, living what he fancied was the life of a normal man in working-class duds. His street, Hauptstrasse, was (and still is) modest, but his apartment there had seven rooms, and his record company offered to helicopter him out and set him up in a mansion if he'd only record something more commercial; so he was kidding himself, just as I was. We were both putting on an act, wearing thin disguises, and creating a character. He was playing 'Bowie in Berlin'. I was playing a hybrid Brooker-Bowie in Berlin, forty years later.

I couldn't stay in his apartment, so I took residence at the Hotel Ellington, formerly the Dschungel, mentioned in 2013's retrospective 'Where Are We Now?' as the club Bowie and Iggy had frequented in the 1970s. I drank his preferred beer, König, at his local gay bar, Anderes Ufer ('the other side', now renamed Neues Ufer), and spent afternoons at the Brücke Museum, looking at the Erich Heckel paintings he'd admired. I even practised my German, which I hadn't used since school.

Inevitably, my project couldn't be a straight translation; not just because I could never be Bowie, but because, like any adaptation, a revisiting of the original is always shaped

by the cultural context. Berlin's geography had been transformed, of course, and it was now an entirely different city
to the one Bowie knew in the 1970s. The wall that had
separated families for decades was now just a marker in the
pavement, with fragments of its graffitied concrete slabs
preserved as memorials at Potsdamer Platz. The guard towers
Bowie had seen from Hansa Studios, inspiring '"Heroes"', had
been torn down. I was able to walk easily across the no-man's-
land where people had once been shot for crossing the border.
My experience involved a double vision: looking at my own
reflection and trying to see Bowie behind it, walking the
streets he'd known and trying to feel him beside me, and
immersing myself in recreations of his experiences while
retaining a sense of myself as observer. As I fumblingly
explained in an interview at the *David Bowie Is* exhibition in
Melbourne, I was 'not trying to become David Bowie, but . . .
to use part of my mind, a kind of satellite of my mind, to
become David Bowie, while the other parts observe that, and
comment on it critically'.

People asked me if I'd reached out to Bowie himself. I
hadn't, but a journalist did. Bowie, or his people, said 'no
comment', which I took as a positive response: his condem-
nation would have been the only thing to make me stop. At
least he'd replied, kind of. I never really expected to meet
him, though of course I entertained fantasies about it, while
he was still alive. I hoped he'd be mildly amused by my

research. It was, after all, the kind of daft thing he'd done when he was around my age: dressing up in Andy Warhol's old outfits and pretending to be one of his own heroes on the streets of New York, as preparation for the 1996 movie *Basquiat*. Prior to that, he'd undertaken intense research to play Joseph ('John') Merrick in *The Elephant Man* on Broadway, studying the subject's clothes and a body mould made after his death; and in the 1960s, as he later admitted, he'd temporarily become another of his idols: 'I was Tony Newley for a year.' (He was 'Anthony Newley's double, really', suggests biographer Wendy Leigh. 'And Newley was furious.')

Some of Bowie's friends, I heard through mutual contacts, were unimpressed, and I could hardly blame them, especially after his death. I wouldn't be happy with some barely talented chancer attempting to 'become' an artist-genius I'd known and loved personally. But while the project had gained international media attention over the summer of 2015, it had started as something small and personal to me – just a springboard to start my research process – and while it had begun as a way to know Bowie better, it became increasingly about getting to know myself, and change myself. The schedule I'd set myself, based on his life, provided a structure of events and exercises I had to undertake; and as I pushed myself through those challenges, I found myself digging back into my own past and pushing my own boundaries. The research was about him, but it was also about me.

As I revisited points in Bowie's life, I inevitably compared them to what I was doing during that year. I hadn't been to Berlin since 1988, when I was a teenager studying German, and the wall was still up. I found some of my set texts from A-level and struggled through them, proud of myself when I managed to read a Max Frisch play in the original language. I unearthed my old cine films and diaries from the time, remembering who I was as an adolescent, and revisiting that period – that person – as well as the city.

As I progressed through my project, my Bowie persona grew older – I began in June 2015, touching base with the twenty-year-old David who'd hung out at the Gioconda and the Marquee, and by September I was emulating the thirty-year-old Bowie of Berlin clubs. By the time I reached *Let's Dance* – which I celebrated by holding an interview session in the cocktail bar at Claridge's; tanned, blond and wearing a suit with broad, padded shoulders – Bowie was in his mid-thirties. When he recorded *The Buddha of Suburbia*, in 1993, he was forty-six, the same age as me in 2016. I laid photos of myself in those key years next to images of Bowie, watching myself grow up and grow older alongside him. Another double vision; another parallel perspective. I was using Bowie's experiences as a framework to look back at my own life, and ask myself what I wanted to be doing with it.

I'd given up a lot since I was eighteen, I realised. Our education system in the UK is focused on narrowing down as we get older, becoming more expert in fewer things, and as a career academic, I'd squeezed myself through that funnel system. As a teenager – even in my early twenties – I'd still sometimes felt free enough to draw, paint and sing, just for the fun of it; to experiment creatively in areas I knew I was never going to follow up professionally. I was fluid with fashion, combining dangly earrings, eyeliner and floral scarves with leather jackets and biker boots. I took the occasional evening class in acting and improvisation. I'd been fluent in French and German, and lived with families in Paris and Berlin. But gradually I let it all go. I gave up foreign languages when I chose a film and English degree at age eighteen, and abandoned filmmaking when I failed, predictably, to break into the industry. I picked up some part-time teaching and found that the preparation, travel and marking took up all my time. I told myself I'd keep up my creative writing, but I was too tired after work.

By my mid-twenties I'd cut almost every creative activity from my life, as I devoted myself to a PhD. Anything surplus was forgotten. Acting and singing weren't going to get me employed. I was never going to be a great artist, but I was becoming a promising academic. I'd learned the lesson that you shouldn't show off your work unless it's above a certain standard. People don't praise a thirty-year-old for a half-decent drawing the way they do a kid at primary school. They're embarrassed. They want you to wait until you're better, and if you don't get better, they'd rather you kept it to yourself, or maybe just stop.

So I concentrated on academic writing, and honed myself to fit specific roles and hit specific targets. I got a PhD. I got a job. I got promotions. As a head of the film department at thirty-five, I couldn't mess around with vintage clothes and make-up. I was expected to wear suits, so I bought a lot of suits. By the time I started my Bowie research, aged forty-five, I'd barely drawn or painted, or sung in public, or performed creatively, or dressed up imaginatively, for twenty years. In a way I'd done well, but I'd also lost a lot of myself.

But now I had to draw on that old energy, and rediscover those half-forgotten, amateur abilities. I'd set myself this project, I'd told the world media about it, and, for my own sake, I didn't want to give up. Each step in Bowie's life presented a new creative challenge. Go to Hastings beach wearing Pierrot make-up. Sing 'Boys Keep Swinging' in drag at one of London's oldest gay clubs. Find your way to an art museum in Berlin. Paint an Expressionist portrait. Front a Bowie tribute band. By attempting to engage with his experiences, I was bringing things from my own past back to the present, and touching base with who I used to be. My matrix was intersecting with his, and the overlaps were making my life richer.

Nobody can become Bowie. But by connecting with him, and trying to immerse myself in his personae, I created a bolder, braver and brighter version of myself. Rather than pretending to be him in my media interviews, I adopted his approach; sometimes accidentally, and sometimes deliberately. I realised that when you're asked the same question six times, you start making up different answers, just to keep yourself entertained. I dropped in a few exaggerations that I knew nobody would check. I changed the narrative. I understood why Bowie came up with his fanciful stories about Brixton, and the ancient farmhouse in Yorkshire, and the album called *The Best Haircut I Ever Had*. There are multiple stories about my research out there (and perhaps also in here) that don't entirely add up. It's hard, even with the best intentions, to remember the exact sequence of events in your own life.

More consciously, I set myself a character note for different interviews, in keeping with Bowie and Brian Eno's use of Oblique Strategy cards – with their gnomic guidance like 'You are an engineer', 'What would your closest friend do?' and 'Use unqualified people' – and their more elaborate approach on 1995's *1. Outside* album.

Eno assigned roles to the band members, offering them flash-cards to shape their studio performances; so Bowie would sing as if he were a village storyteller, for instance, while Mike Garson was told to approach his piano as if he were the commander of a lost starship. One card read: 'You are a disgruntled ex-member of a South African rock band. Play the notes you were not allowed to play.' I went into interviews with similar, self-imposed aims, to explore the dynamic between myself and the media. In one, I resolved to claim I saw no difference now between myself and Bowie, and that I planned to replace him. In the next, I based my behaviour on both David Frost and Richard Nixon in their televised verbal duels of 1977. I knew the interviewer would try to ridicule and embarrass me, so I got my moves in first, trying to keep him off-balance.

I became far more confident than I would have dared if I was appearing simply under my own name. I wasn't simply myself now, but a concept called 'The Bowie Professor'. Journalists would start the conversation by asking who exactly they were speaking to, as if I were channelling another persona, much as Bowie did at the height of his own immersion in the Ziggy Stardust character. I was performing as an overlap between myself – my old self, perhaps, that more experimental and creative self – and my personal interpretation of David Bowie. It was an exhausting, but in many ways, a liberating experience. You can't go through that and not be changed. And once you've completed those challenges, it's hard to look back.

When my research year ended in May 2016, I wanted to achieve closure without leaving behind what I'd learned from the project. I wanted to be fully myself again, but to retain the changes I'd taken from my twelve months of 'being Bowie'. I went for six sessions with a therapist, in a deliberate move to build a bridge out of the immersion, back into something more like everyday life. We discussed the process of mourning I'd gone through for Bowie. I'm sure many fans experienced the same, whether or not they ever met him. We talked about the repression that, she argued, shapes my generation and the one before it; she felt that it all went back to the Second World War. Children were born into households that had experienced terror and loss; fathers came back to their families having seen, and done, things they never wanted to speak about again.

Bowie, born in 1947, grew up in this environment. His father had fought in North Africa and Italy, then bought the house on Stansfield Road because the area was so cheap; the German bombs had hit Brixton hard. There were gaps in the rows of terraced houses, and bombsites covered with struggling flowers. Rationing was firmly in place when David was young, with shop window displays and illuminated signs still forbidden under old blackout rules.

We gained a sense from the first chapter of how stultifying and confined his later childhood and adolescence in Bromley might have been: the little terraced house, the identical neighbours – morning, Miss West, good morning, Mr Hall – the cold room with the tuna sandwiches, the parents who struggled to openly show affection. Millions of parents – or this was my therapist's theory, anyway – had grown up in a similar cage of middle-class convention and repression, in a country that was trying to recover from the collective trauma of war by locking emotion away. Those parents, she said, passed the same culture of containment to their children – David's generation – who unwittingly passed it down, in turn, to mine. 'Man hands on misery to man,' as Philip Larkin put it. David Jones resisted in the 1960s, and in the early 1970s David Bowie broke free. He was a one-man carnival, setting an example of what you could do if you refused the rules and ignored what people thought of you. I'd tapped into some of that energy, and felt its potential.

The challenge was how to preserve that 'Bowieness', while stepping back from the immersion: how to keep the energy, but make it my own, rather than imitating him. Again, the answer comes back to adaptation. I'd started the year by attempting a faithful translation. During the process, my own history and experience had merged with his matrix, and I moved away from the intense immersion, but I was still using his life as a template and a framework, even in the final months of my research. The way forward lay in a much looser adaptation, more like Bowie's approach to *Nineteen Eighty-Four*. Instead of copying him, I would draw on his influence – as he did with his inspirations, like Lou Reed and Bob Dylan – and combine it more consciously with elements from my own personal warehouse: masks, voices, costumes from my imaginary museum.

So I deliberately assembled styles inspired by Bowie, but

which he'd never adopted himself. My celebrity dressmaker put together a jacket with silver stars; an upbeat, summery response to Bowie's *Blackstar* from the previous January. The hairdresser who'd taken me through changes from *'Heroes'* to *Earthling* to *Reality* gave me a blond cut with a tangerine-coloured fringe, the inverse of *The Man Who Fell to Earth*. I kept the eye make-up and nail varnish, and combined them with suits in teal and purple, and a fistful of chunky jewellery. People told me I looked like Nick Rhodes, from Duran Duran. That was fine by me. I'd succeeded in moving away from Bowie, even if I was now paying accidental tribute to another of my 1980s icons.

I started drumming again – something I'd given up at age ten – because it was one instrument Bowie hadn't played. I kept up the singing lessons and the drawing classes, and I got better at both; I'm never going to be professional at either, but I can compare what I'm able to do now with what I managed a few years ago, and see how much I've improved. I occasionally perform live at local pubs, just as Bowie did at the Three Tuns in the late 1960s. It was the start of his career as a musician, and it's going to be as far as I get, but that's fine.

Even now, I often ask myself, 'What would Bowie do?', calling on him as a symbolic guide and mentor. There are worse ways to live your life. But alongside Bowie, another of my inspirations is the thirteen-year-old I used to be, who imagined whole worlds from 'Ricochet', a track on the B-side of his mum's music cassette, and took the bus to Lewisham Shopping Centre to find the jacket that came closest to his vision. At thirteen, I was doing something similar to Bowie when he invented Ziggy Stardust: creating my own character, who was bigger and bolder than myself, and trying to become him.

This, I now think – and I speak with some experience – is the way to adapt Bowie into your own life: not to copy him directly and specifically, but to follow his broader example, and allow his matrix of ideas and influences to mesh with your own. Nobody can become Bowie, but we can all become a little *more* Bowie; we can all incorporate a bit of Bowie into our lives. Draw on your own wonder-house of experiences to dream up a version of yourself – perhaps more colourful, more creative, more confident – and then inhabit it, and see what happens. It worked for him. It worked for me.

3

CHANGING

My immersive research ended in May 2016, and the following September I was asked to teach a class on Bowie at Kingston University. Technically, the subject was celebrity, but inevitably Bowie was my starting point. It was an intensive, research-based module, with a small group of dedicated students. They were all about twenty years old: confidently experimental with their clothes, hair and make-up, and as open about their gender identity, sexuality and mental health as they were about their favourite films and music. They came to Bowie with open minds, but without much prior knowledge. They acknowledged him as an icon, but he was a figure from their dads' generation at best. They were born at the end of the

1990s, and the image they associated with him – Aladdin Sane, with scarlet lightning flashing across his pale face – dated from 1973, over a quarter of a century earlier.

I was hoping to gently convince them of Bowie's influence and continued relevance. Articles after his death, earlier that year, had praised him as a genderqueer pioneer who'd been 'flying the flag for the non-binary movement' since the 1970s, and who 'still represents a queer ideal that's playful, sex-positive, and devoid of labels'. I was expecting these young people to tolerate my own Bowie fandom, then move on to explore their own independent topics. I wasn't expecting any of them to reject Bowie by the second week of semester.

We'd spent the first session discussing the notorious racial stereotypes in the 'China Girl' video from 1983, and moved on to issues of sexuality. I introduced the class to two contro-versial quotations, eleven years apart. In 1972, Bowie told the *Melody Maker*, 'I'm gay and I always have been, even when I was David Jones.' In 1983, by contrast, he confided to *Rolling Stone* that 'the biggest mistake I ever made was telling that *Melody Maker* writer that I was bisexual.' One of my students, a young man studying film and fashion, threw up his hands in frustration. 'Can we stop talking about David Bowie? He's making me so angry! The more I know about him, the angrier I get!' I invited him to say more. 'He's just using gay culture to market himself. All he ever seems to do is steal from other people.'

The student went on to design a jacket for his assessed piece. In his critical commentary, he explained, with the same engaging annoyance, that the piece had become the bane of his life and that the sleeves had fallen off before he submitted the work. He got a First for that class, despite the sleeves, and graduated in summer 2017. Ironically, he reminded me of the young David Bowie, whose customised corduroy jacket with inked pinstripes is now on display in Bromley Library: they were both energetic, impatient and creative. I don't know what that student is doing now, but his words have stuck with me. I'm grateful to him for the reminder that our heroes are far from perfect, and that they made mistakes and missteps, too. Bowie, who placed inverted commas firmly around 'Heroes', would surely have agreed.

My student was far from the first to feel disillusioned by Bowie's apparent denial of his bisexuality, not to mention his clumsy explorations of racial and cultural identity. Chris O'Leary accuses the 1980s Bowie of being an 'opportunist', repudiating gay men after 'he had trafficked in their culture, had pretended (even claimed) to be one for several years.' Mitchell Plitnick's article 'We Can Be Heroes' describes Bowie's *Rolling Stone* interview as a 'really devastating moment'. John Gill's book *Queer Noises* scathingly calls Bowie a 'consummate self-publicist' whose gayness was 'just another role'; in David Buckley's words, Bowie comes across as 'a closet homophobe who cynically manipulated his own sexuality'.

Lev Raphael's short story 'Betrayed by David Bowie' condemns his 1983 incarnation for 'claiming to be just like everyone else . . . "The Man Who Sold the World" was selling himself and everyone who'd believed in him.'

From these accounts, Bowie had given up all his queerness – in every sense – by the release of *Let's Dance*, and adopted a safe, heterosexual conformity: the power to subvert was replaced by, in the words of 'Modern Love', 'just the power to charm'. Buckley summarises his press conference appearance at Claridge's in March 1983: 'He was now the concerned white liberal; the anxious father; the suavely manicured, old-fashioned superstar; the song-and-dance man and the svelte son-of-Sinatra.' Ten years after the release of *Aladdin Sane*, the pale alien had come firmly down to earth, acquiring immaculate suits and a tasteful suntan. This was a new persona for the mainstream MTV era, primed for Pepsi commercials with Tina Turner. As he half promised, half warned in 'China Girl', on the same album, 'I'll give you television, I'll give you eyes of blue. I'll give you the man who wants to rule the world.' He'd come out as a sell-out.

But in the month of his death, as mentioned above, the artist who'd apparently lost his radical credibility by the mid-eighties was praised again as a pioneer. He was, Heather Saul explained in the *Independent*, an inspiration to the androgynous rock star Marilyn Manson, to genderfluid actor and activist Ruby Rose, and to transgender supermodel Andreja Pejic, who 'thanked Bowie for breaking boundaries decades ago with transgressive, non-conformist work'. Christina Cauterucci, in *Slate*, argued that Bowie had refused to be pinned down by labels of gay, straight and bisexual, and that his 'androgynous legacy finds new footing in gender-bending celebrities like Jaden Smith'. More recently yet, in January 2018, journalist Sally Kohn reinterpreted Bowie's *Rolling Stone* repudiation of his earlier bisexual 'mistake' not as a betrayal, but as an admirable 'searching . . . illustrating a fluidity of sexuality that many still have trouble grasping'. 'Let's face it,' Kohn suggests, 'David Bowie might have been the world's first transgender ally – before we had words like "transgender" or even "ally" in our vernacular. He was also one of the first famous gay allies.'

How can we reconcile these apparent contradictions: a man who supposedly sold out to straight superstardom in 1983, but who also served as a role model for genderqueer activists like Ruby Rose (born in 1986)? Was Bowie's bisexuality of the early 1970s just a pose, an experiment, or a superficial appropriation from a genuinely oppressed group? Should we see his shifting statements about his own sexuality between 1972 and 1983 as a commercially safe, politically conservative attempt to distance himself from his earlier, bolder claims, or as a reflection of his genuinely felt fluidity? Was he a betrayer of gay culture, or 'one of the first famous gay allies'? Was he 'the world's first transgender ally', a genderqueer pioneer, or, as my student felt, a cynical thief? Did he redeem himself, or simply explain himself, between the 1983 interview and the end of his career?

Should we, in turn, separate Bowie's experiments with gendered presentation – his drag, make-up and androgynous outfits – from his changing claims about his sexual preferences? Heather Saul's *Independent* article concludes with a quotation from Stonewall, celebrating Bowie as 'a vibrant and visible icon who has done so much for the lesbian, gay, bi and trans community in both his art and his actions'. We readily use 'LGBT' now (and longer versions of the initialism) as an umbrella term, but neither Bowie, nor his fans, nor the music press would have understood it in the 1970s. Sexuality and gender identity are now considered as quite separate, but when Bowie made those claims, they were often confused and conflated: to be a 'feminine' man, wearing dresses or make-up, or even just long hair, was to signal that you were gay. 'Ally', of course, would have been more likely to signify the troops who fought the Nazis than a friend to oppressed minorities.

Similarly, while individuals have embodied 'non-binary' and 'genderqueer' approaches in diverse cultural contexts throughout history, the terms themselves are relatively recent. Bowie associated closely with transgender women in the mid-1970s, but neither he nor they would have used that word at the time. Even 'bisexual' had subtly different connotations from its current meaning, as we'll see. Does it make sense to apply our own vocabulary and values retrospectively to Bowie's early career, or do we need to understand what his 'art and his actions' would have meant in their original context?

Well, yes and no, or as James Joyce usefully put it in *Ulysses*, 'Nes. Yo.' Two things can be more or less equally true at the same time. As I suggested in the previous chapter, our understanding of Bowie and his work can be independent of his original intention. *Let's Dance*, seen as the start of Bowie's 1980s artistic decline by many critics, marked the beginning of my fandom. He might have meant it as a shift towards the commercial mainstream, but I experienced that album as vivid, evocative and inventive. A Bowie song is a shared creation between him and us, and we are, I've argued, all entitled to our own interpretations and personal associations.

We rarely restrict our interpretations of Bowie's music to what we know he meant in 1973, or 1985, or 1997: to paraphrase Roland Barthes again, we do not tend to receive each Bowie song as a message handed down by the Author-God, to be decoded for its underlying truth. His work is rich, complex and alive – and it will stay vibrantly alive – partly because of what we invest in it from our own experience. If we want to trace a lineage from Aladdin Sane to Jaden Smith, and identify Bowie as genderqueer at a time before the word existed, that's one valid way to join up dots and make links; to connect points into a new pattern, however ahistorical.

Barthes's 'Death of the Author' argument – that meaning resides in us, the reader, rather than the creator – is, then, not just a theoretical notion for seminar rooms and university classes. We can see it clearly in the way people have responded to Bowie's work, disregarding what he intended and focusing instead on its effect. Bowie's message in the 'China Girl' video was, he explained in the infamous *Rolling Stone* interview, simply that 'it's wrong to be racist!', but whatever irony he meant to invest in the video's visual imagery was lost on (or irrelevant to) Asian-American academic Ellie M. Hisama, who saw the song as reinforcing 'a pernicious racial and sexual stereotype that many of us have to live within'.

On the other hand, John Gill suggests that while gayness was 'just another role' for Bowie, the pose nevertheless achieved a positive result: 'He did not necessarily help shape my sexuality, but his high-profile example created a breathing space both for queers and for those who weren't sure about their sexuality.' As Tom Robinson confirmed: 'For gay musicians, Bowie was seismic . . . to hell with whether he disowned us later.' Boy George agreed. 'Bowie gave me permission to be me. He validated me, he allowed me to be different and to embrace that difference.' Many other musicians who grew up with his music in the 1970s – Marc Almond, Robert Smith, Siouxsie Sioux – offer similar testimonies: whatever

Bowie's intentions, he liberated them from sexual and gender conformity. His influence went beyond what we would now call the LGBT community; he also inspired straight artists who challenged convention in their style and presentation, like Ian McCulloch from Echo and the Bunnymen. 'With people like me,' said McCulloch, 'it helped forge an identity and a perspective on things – helped us to walk in a different way, metaphorically, and to see things differently.' Whatever else, Bowie matters simply because of this 'seismic' effect on his fans: celebrities and otherwise.

On the one hand, then, intention is irrelevant. The meaning of a Bowie text rests with us, the people who receive it: so, even a cynical appropriation of gay culture can open doors for others, while a naïve attempt to condemn racism can unwittingly confirm racial stereotypes. But the other, it's also helpful to know what shaped Bowie's artistic statements, and to reconstruct the social and cultural context around them.

Bowie's ability to deftly play with gender and sexual roles had emerged clearly by the time he was seventeen. In November 1964, drumming up publicity for his Society for the Prevention of Cruelty to Long-Haired Men, he landed an interview on BBC2's *Tonight* show. 'I think we're all fairly tolerant,' the fresh-faced Davie Jones protested from beneath his blond fringe. 'But for the last two years we've had comments like "Darling", and "Can I carry your handbag?" thrown at us. I think it's just had to stop now.' The interviewer, Cliff Michelmore, asked, 'But does this surprise you, that you get this kind of comment?' As Bowie fully understood, long hair on young men was associated with femininity, and in turn, implied homosexuality. He played with the idea in a push-pull provocation, courting controversy while also seeming to condemn it. It was meant more as a publicity stunt than a genuine protest about restrictive sexual and gender roles. As Bowie subsequently boasted, 'My girlfriend isn't keen on my hair either. Maybe it's because I get asked on more dates when we're out together.'

Two months later, during an audition for a The Manish Boys booking, the promoter asked David – now just turned eighteen – if he preferred girls or boys. 'Boys, of course,' was the reply. 'He was just putting the guy on,' said his bandmate Paul Rodriguez. 'We'd say anything to get a good gig.' Bowie later claimed, in a *Playboy* interview from 1976, that he'd been actively bisexual from the age of fourteen. 'It didn't really matter who or what it was with, as long as it was a sexual experience. So it was some very pretty boy in class in some school or other that I took home and neatly fucked on my bed upstairs.'

This bold, but typically vague claim ('some school or other') seems improbable to say the least, and it also contradicts the testimonies of Bowie's school-friends. The Konrads guitarist

Alan Dodds remembers Bowie claiming 'he was bisexual, but I have to say there was absolutely no evidence for that. I think he was just up for anything that was a bit different.' Brian Bough, his classmate from Bromley Tech, went on holiday with David and his parents in Great Yarmouth when they were fifteen, and remembers not only that both boys were exclusively interested in girls, but that they enjoyed very little success. Bowie apparently had more luck by 1965, at age seventeen: Phil Lancaster, drummer in the Lower Third, told biographer Wendy Leigh that he 'had no doubts what-soever that David was heterosexual', based on their shared gigging experiences that year.

However, the band's manager, Ralph Horton, was both 'relatively open about being gay' and 'enthralled by David', according to Lancaster and his fellow musicians: after a few months on the road, Bowie began travelling to and from gigs in Horton's Jaguar, rather than loading up the ambulance, and the two would sometimes share a room. 'There was no point getting uptight,' said Derek Boyes, keyboard player from the Buzz. 'In the business, agents, impresarios, ninety-nine percent of them were bent anyway.' Whatever happened behind closed doors on tour, Bowie went to great lengths to tease his manager: Leni and Peter Gillman recount a story about Bowie turning up late at Horton's place 'in full drag, wearing make-up and a ball gown'. 'Miss Garland is here,' his chauffeur announced.

He played a similar game with his first solo manager, Ken Pitt. Then in his forties, Pitt was a campaigner for homosexual law reform, but discreet about his own sexuality when Bowie moved into an apartment with him in June 1967. Bowie, who at this time was mixing with openly gay men in the theatrical scene – he began training with Lindsay Kemp that autumn, and was apparently doted on by Lionel Bart, creator of *Oliver!* – knew how to press his new mentor's buttons. 'He arrived one morning in Pitt's office with his hair piled in curls,' and started to perform 'stagey feminine mannerisms, fluttering his eyelids and crossing his legs when he sat down', Peter and Leni Gillman report. 'Pitt pretended not to notice.'

Pitt's autobiography confirms that he did notice, though: he noticed every detail. 'I could see that he was wearing a biscuit-coloured, hand-knitted sweater,' Pitt wrote of one meeting, 'round-necked and buttoned at one shoulder, its skin-tightness accentuating his slim frame.' Another description ventures further: 'David derived comfort from leaving off his clothes, sometimes sitting cross-legged on the floor encircled by blaring hi-fi speakers, sometimes loping around the flat, naked, his long, weighty penis swaying from side to side like the pendulum of a grandfather clock.'

Those who knew him in 1967 suggest that Bowie certainly experimented with other men, but that the relationships were unbalanced, and that his motivation may have been cynical. 'David was bisexual, but was predominantly heterosexual,' said Jonathan King, then a young singer-songwriter like Bowie. 'Looking back now, I've got the feeling that his gay experiences were part of wanting to get on.' George Tremlett, who saw Bowie and his manager together at their Manchester Street apartment, concludes that 'Pitt genuinely loved him, but Bowie was always a chancer . . . Pitt was left in no doubt that Bowie would happily sleep with women as well.' One evening, Bowie brought a girl back from a party, and Pitt interrupted them, telling her it was time to leave: Bowie chased down the stairs after her, but Pitt grabbed his arm. 'You're too bloody possessive,' Bowie protested, as the young woman vanished into the London night.

There were similar melodramatic scenes with Lindsay Kemp later that year, when the mime tutor found Bowie's shoes outside the bedroom door of his costumier, Natasha Korniloff. 'He's my boyfriend!' Kemp cried. 'No, he's mine!' replied Korniloff. Again, whatever relationship Kemp and Bowie had was unbalanced, with Bowie apparently in the role of the ambitious grifter, prepared to swing with older guys if they offered him a career boost. 'We mucked about a little,' says Kemp. 'He really thought that music had given him up. He wasn't getting anywhere when I met him.' In an echo of Ken Pitt's unrequited affections, Kemp mused that 'I don't think his love was as deep as mine . . . there were always lots of other women.'

Bowie broke everyone's heart again a few days later when

he met Hermione Farthingale, credited in Kevin Cann's chronology of Bowie's early life as his 'first mature relationship'. There's a striking contrast between these fully-documented romances with women, and the ambiguity that still surrounds Bowie's involvement with his male mentors. Whether Horton and Bowie ever did more than share a room comes down to decades-old gossip; the story about Bowie turning up in Judy Garland drag, while entertaining, is an unsupported, isolated anecdote. Similarly, biographers have to read between the lines of the teasing and squabbling to deduce that Pitt never actually slept with Bowie; and even Kemp's memories of the time are coy, with their brief mention of 'mucking about a little'. Bowie himself is, as we might expect, the only source of the story about the fourteen-year-old boy.

We can only guess at his motivations, but, as in the first chapter, we can identify his patterns of behaviour from the available facts. The overriding impression is of Bowie toying with feminine presentation and hinting at gayness, partly for its shock and publicity value, and then beginning to experiment with bisexuality. Obsessed with success by almost any means necessary, he was clearly prepared to at least tolerate the romantic attention of older men, bending it to his own ends, but he also used his androgyny to attract younger girls who, unlike Horton and Pitt, couldn't offer him any career advantages. Dana Gillespie was captivated by his long blond hair, and claims that her father 'didn't know whether David was a man or a woman until he opened his mouth'. She was 'a very forward fourteen-year-old girl', she says, when she invited David back from the Marquee to her parents' house: it's not impossible that Bowie remembered her story, switched the sexes and retold it as his own true (false) confession to *Playboy*, years later.

Bowie's bisexuality was, on this evidence, more of a side gig: a hustle he was using to get ahead. He knew he was attractive to men like Horton, Pitt and Kemp, who had contacts and connections; he enjoyed being idolised, and he liked what it did for his career, but he seems to have held back from becoming physically – let alone emotionally – involved with them. But the fact that the truth remains so elusive is also telling. From the multiple biographies, chronologies and testimonies of Bowie's early life, we can build up a detailed picture of his teenage dates with Dana Gillespie, from their first meeting and sexual encounter to their lasting friendship and, in her words, 'musical relationship'. The same books give us only an uncertain sense of how far he went with Horton, Pitt and Kemp.

Similarly, we can easily learn every detail about Bowie's brief relationship with his landlady Mary Finnigan – how she first heard him playing guitar from her upstairs window, how he won her over with a candlelit dinner, a bottle of wine and a nest of cushions on the bedroom floor, and how she reacted to finding Angela Barnett in her kitchen one morning. We can reconstruct every intimate aspect of Bowie's relationship with Angie, too, from their first night together to their wedding outfits and their divorce settlement. But Mary Finnigan, who lived with Bowie between April and October 1969, 'wasn't really aware of him with other men'. Her recollection that Bowie was involved with Lindsay Kemp, Lionel Bart and Mercury Records man Calvin Mark Lee is all based on second-hand information rather than her first-hand memories. She makes sense of it, in retrospect, by supposing she must have been 'very naïve': 'I didn't clock it at the time.'

Angie was also enjoying a fling with Calvin Mark Lee, who took her to the Feathers performance where she first saw David. Her boast that 'when we met, we were both fucking the same bloke' is a typical Bowie soundbite, combining deliberate provocation with liberated cool, but again, we only have marginal details about Lee's affair with David. Biographer Marc Spitz interviewed him for four hours, and reports that 'we spoke of David Bowie for twenty minutes'. His mention of the overlapping flings with Angie and David is extremely brief, and far tamer than Angie's phrasing. 'I was having an affair with Angie. And I did introduce her to him at the Roundhouse. So we were going around with the same person.'

Again, we can see a pattern emerging: the same push-pull dynamic that Bowie carefully played with Horton, Kemp and Pitt. 'Maybe,' Lee considered, 'he needed something at the time, which was fine with me . . . one doesn't mind being used if there's a feeling the other way.' We might also note that Lee, like Lindsay Kemp, was about a decade older than Bowie. Marc Spitz notes that 'like Bowie, Lee was open to bisexual experiences', but while Lee says his preferences are 'five percent girls and ninety-five percent boys', Bowie's ratio at the time seems skewed in the other direction. Based on what we can piece together from these memoirs, Bowie seems to have treated bisexuality a little like mime or Buddhism: a fashionable idea that tempted him for a while; a new hobby to pursue more or less enthusiastically while he assessed how it could help his career.

We could argue, though, that while some of these recollections are relatively recent – Lee was interviewed by Marc Spitz in 2008 – there will inevitably be less detailed evidence of male–male relationships in the late 1960s compared to heterosexual romances. Bowie may have enjoyed dropping hints about his open-minded preferences, but others – those for whom gayness was more than a hobby – were far more careful, and for good reason. To reconstruct the context of Bowie's 1972 *Melody Maker* interview, we have to consider not just the events of his life that led up to it, but also the cultural and political environment.

Even in their 1986 biography, Peter and Leni Gilman only hint at Ken Pitt's homosexuality through coded references to his 'orderly, discreet' decor 'that revealed a taste for the mannered and aesthetic life of the late nineteenth century'.

'Among them were Aubrey Beardsley, Lord Alfred Douglas and – his favourite – Oscar Wilde . . . Pitt had strong sympathy for the plight of homosexual men in post-war Britain, still stigmatised for their sexual preferences, and still liable, even at the beginning of 1967, to legal penalties for indulging in them.'

As they note, it was only thirteen years earlier, in 1954, that Lord Edward Montagu had been sentenced to a year in prison for homosexual offences, alongside his friend, and Ken Pitt's cousin, Michael Pitt-Rivers. Montagu had reported a stolen camera to the police and been investigated for his private life; if police suspected a man was gay, they would disregard the original crime, and charge the victim for his personal activities. Alan Turing had a similar experience when he reported a break-in, in 1952: the subsequent conviction for gross indecency led to his suicide.

It was cases of this kind that prompted the UK government to establish the Wolfenden Committee, which in 1957 recommended that 'homosexual behaviour between consenting adults in private should no longer be a criminal offence'; but the progress from this decision to the subsequent Sexual Offences Act, which put its recommendation into legal practice, took a full decade. Lawyer Leo Abse, who steered the change to the law through Parliament, remembers Wolfenden as 'not by any means a key turning-point. Ten years of struggle came after.'

In 1958, reports novelist and *Observer* journalist Geraldine

Bedell in an *Observer* article on the anniversary of the Wolfenden Report, 'there would be intermittent trawls through address books of suspected homosexuals, with the result that up to twenty men at a time would appear in the dock, accused of being a "homosexual ring", even though many of them might never have met many of the others.' The Homosexual Law Reform Society was set up in the same year, calling for the implementation of Wolfenden's recommendations: its secretary, Anthony Grey, waited until he was thirty to tell his parents he was gay, 'and they thought it was some foul disease'.

During the 1960s, according to campaigner Peter Tatchell, debates concerning changes to the law around homosexuality 'alternated between vicious homophobia on one side and patronising, apologetic tolerance on the other'. Even the campaign's supporters, Leo Abse recalled, saw gay men as pitiful and in need of charity: 'Look, these people, these gays, poor gays, they can't have a wife, they can't have children, it's a terrible life.' The implementation of the law in 1967 finally made same-sex relations legal in private, but any arrangements made in public were still a crime: two men chatting each other up in a park, or exchanging numbers on the street, were 'soliciting' or 'procuring'.

This background puts Bowie's provocations in a different light. He was born, we should remember, two decades before homosexuality was even legalised as a private activity. David

Jones had grown up in a period when gay men were witch-hunted by the police and victims of crime were prosecuted as criminals for their private life, their offences considered too disgraceful to be reported as anything more specific than 'gross indecency'. His knowing suggestions about his own sexual fluidity were entirely out of keeping with the dominant cultural mood; for a teenager in the first half of the 1960s, they were boldly ahead of their time.

He was openly claiming to prefer boys to girls in 1964, when the first gay rights groups were just beginning to emerge – the Campaign for Homosexual Equality was established in the same year as Bowie's Society for the Prevention of Cruelty to Long-Haired Men. The previous year, as Hugh David discusses in his book *On Queer Street*, the *Sunday Mirror* had still felt it necessary to offer a two-page guide on 'How to Spot a Possible Homo' ('shifty glances . . . dropped eyes . . . a fondness for the theatre').

Gay culture – or as it was called, 'the homosexual problem' – sneaked into the mainstream during the 1960s through political discussion, comedy shows (like Bowie's favourite *Round the Horne*) and popular studies, and was starting to prompt distanced interest rather than automatic revulsion and alarm, but Bowie's behaviour nevertheless went against the flow: he embodied not just tolerance or curiosity, but an easy-going acceptance of gayness that Britain as a whole would not embrace for decades.

He moved in with Ken Pitt a month before the Sexual Offences Act decriminalised homosexual acts in private between men over the age of twenty-one: as Bowie was still twenty years old, Pitt would have been guilty of gross indecency for any sexual contact between them, and liable to a sentence of up to five years. No wonder Pitt tried to ignore the teasing, and no surprise, perhaps, that the older men in Bowie's life – Horton, Pitt, Kemp and Lee – were all careful about taking Bowie up on his flirtatious advances, and cagey about recording the details of their affairs with him.

Even if he'd kept his mouth shut, Bowie's long hair, feminine mannerisms and occasional drag would have coded him as gay. He'd proposed to the Lower Third in 1965 that they wear make-up on stage; Phil Lancaster was enthusiastic, thinking that David meant 'clown make-up', but when the band realised what he had in mind, they rejected the idea. 'Not fucking likely,' decided bassist Graham Rivens from the front of the ambulance. That kind of make-up was thought to go hand-in-hand with homosexuality: Wolfenden's son Jeremy was gay, and was warned, once the committee began its work, not to be seen around his father wearing lipstick, as it could have undermined progress towards reform. We'll return to the perceived associations between femininity and gayness in the 1960s and early 1970s, later.

In this context, Bowie's provocations seem less like cynical, casual teasing; or not just like cynical, casual teasing, as both things can be true at the same time. Established professionals like Horton, Pitt and Kemp could help him climb the next rung of his career, but any association with homosexuality could also have been a disaster for his professional reputation. Bowie was chasing popular chart success, not just a regular spot in Soho. He was appearing in mainstream magazines, marketed for teenage girls. Whatever his motives, his bold personal statements about his bisexuality – directly, in interviews, and by implication through the way he dressed and acted – were also professionally risky, culturally subversive, and in a climate where winking at another man could get you arrested, politically radical. Was he just flirting superficially with gayness? Nes. Yo.

The first gay lifestyle magazine, launched in 1969, was, like Wolfenden's son, called *Jeremy*. That it's described by Richard Dyer in *The Culture of Queers* as a 'bisexual' magazine, and that its slogan on the cover of issue 2, 'gay power to the gay people', appears in hot pink between the naked torsos of a man and a woman, confirms the ambiguity around the two terms at the time.

Artist and designer John Coulthart, in his discussion of the magazine's history, suggests that this confusion may have been deliberate: bisexuality was 'a kind of fig leaf', a way to smuggle homosexuality under the radar, and Dyer's use of quotation marks around the word may be arch acknowledgement of that disguise. (*Jeremy*'s advertising slogan – 'the magazine for people who don't care about sex!' – was no doubt another cheeky decoy.) Publishers, Coulthart notes, still had to tread carefully, even two years after the Sexual Offences Act of 1967. David Bowie, interviewed by *Jeremy* in 1970, also trod carefully.

'No sign of David,' writes Tim Hughes, in the January issue of the magazine. 'He's just popped down to the shops for paraffin, and meat for the night's stew.' This sense of the star as a practical, hands-on homemaker is followed by confirmations of his open-minded attitudes, and suggestive hints about where his interests lie. When David returns to Haddon Hall, presumably carrying the paraffin and meat, he shows Hughes around the garden and then takes him to an Oxford Street club. The crowd is sprinkled with 'boys in bone-tight velvet pants held up by redundant broad leather belts whose heavy ornate buckles force one's eyes to midriff level'. The girls – groupies with 'deader than deadpan faces' – outnumber the boys, standing 'in predatory clusters . . . it's just not David's scene'.

'I am a loner. I don't feel the need for conventional relationships,' David explains. 'I was madly in love last year but the gigs got in the way.' In fact, he'd moved into Haddon Hall with Angie in August of the previous year, so he may have been temporarily erasing his own heterosexual relationship for *Jeremy*'s gay readership: another example of his willingness to rewrite even recent history to suit his current audience. 'I don't want to be a leader,' he went on. 'After all, who wants to be a cause?' As Simon Reynolds notes in *Shock and Awe: Glam Rock and Its Legacy*, the article 'presented the singer as very much "on our side", without printing anything like a definitive declaration of his orientation'. Tim Hughes certainly approved: 'David is a refreshing change from many of the inarticulate and untalented charlatans currently littering the world of pop.'

More hints followed: in an April 1971 interview for *Rolling Stone*, Bowie advised journalist John Mendelsohn to 'tell your readers that they can make their minds up about me when I begin getting adverse publicity: when I'm found in bed with Raquel Welsh's husband.' The same piece reports Bowie's claim that his last album was 'about his experiences as a shaven-headed transvestite'. But, as Reynolds observes, 'these were flippant, jesting remarks, and hardly anyone had noticed.' Bowie had encountered a drawback to his constant teasing: people were getting used to it and treating it as a joke. It was losing its power to shock. The *Melody Maker* interview was his attempt to abandon ambiguity and cut straight to the point, in a magazine with an estimated readership of one million each week.

The article was published on 22 January 1972, under the title 'Oh You Pretty Thing', and written by Michael Watts. Like Hughes in *Jeremy*, Watts sets the tone with detailed physical descriptions reminiscent of Ken Pitt's memoirs. 'Even though he wasn't wearing silken gowns right out of Liberty's, and his long blond hair no longer fell wavily past his shoulders, David Bowie was looking yummy.' This extended opening paragraph on David's clothes and how much of his physique they expose concludes: 'I wish you could have been there to varda him; he was so super.' The use of the gay slang term for 'see' (in the language Polari, or Palare) is, of course, carefully chosen, and Bowie rises to this invitation. Their interaction is wry, like music-hall banter. '"Why aren't you wearing your girl's dress today?" I said to him (he has no monopoly on tongue-in-cheek humour). "Oh dear," he replied. "You must understand that it's not a woman's. It's a man's dress."'

And in the middle of this exchange, the bombshell. 'I'm gay . . . and always have been, even when I was David Jones.' It sounds like a simple, straightforward statement, but even within the context of the interview there are nudges and winks, and multiple opportunities to dodge and deny. 'There's a sly jollity about how he says it,' Watts adds, 'a secret smile at the corners of his mouth. He knows that in these times it's permissible to act like a male tart.' Watts, for all his flirtatious to-and-fro, sees right through Bowie, and knows that his personae are often temporary. 'David's present image is to come on like a swishy queen, a gorgeously effeminate boy. He's as camp as a row of tents, with his limp hand and trolling vocabulary.' So yes, he's currently gay, but it's just his 'present image', a 'come on'. Watts, in fact, anticipates our modern word for this kind of cynical manipulation; we still call it 'trolling'. His final line is an appeal for the readership not to accept Bowie despite his gayness, but to try to see a more worthwhile artist beyond the throwaway jokes. 'Don't dismiss David Bowie as a serious musician just because he likes to put us all on a little.'

So the landmark interview – 'almost certainly the most famous David Bowie interview ever published', says Sean Egan, who reproduces it in *Bowie on Bowie* – is in fact more nuanced than its reputation suggests. Watts's scepticism contributes a sense of caution throughout, but Bowie's statement, 'I'm gay,' was also surprisingly open to interpretation. Watts immediately suggests that it's synonymous with 'male tart', for instance; an association that would be lost on us now.

Richard Dyer notes that 'the term "gay" was certainly well established in queer sub-cultural (and therefore certainly Hollywood) circles by the 1930s,' but it took decades for this meaning to reach mainstream Britain. Justin Bengry, writing on 'pre-decriminalisation' gay culture, agrees that 'the term "gay" . . . imported from the United States, was largely unknown in mainstream British English until the late 1960s . . . "gay" was only widely adopted in Britain with the organisation of the Gay Liberation Front in 1970.' 'Among queer men and others in the know,' says Bengry, the word 'gay' had been 'used to reference homosexuality even in the UK for at least the previous two decades'. But a survey of both the liberal British broadsheet the *Guardian*, and the more conservative *Times* newspaper, suggests that the idea of gay culture was still new in the early 1970s, and that even the word itself was more commonly used in its old-fashioned sense of 'happy' or 'bright'.

A *Guardian* article from June 1970, reporting on a 'Gay Lib' protest march in New York's Central Park, explains that the word 'means what it has meant in America for a generation: peculiar, queer, of homosexual inclination'. The fact that it needs to be translated for British readers, though – the writer, Alistair Cooke, describes the march as an 'extraordinary' sight, 'so wild a fantasia that even lifelong New Yorkers wondered whether they'd seen it or dreamed it' – demonstrates the novelty of both the word 'gay' in this sense, and the concept of gay rights in general. The Stonewall protests had only taken place a year before, in June 1969, and another two years would pass before the first major gay demonstration in London, on 1 July 1972 (again, chosen as the closest date to the Stonewall anniversary).

By January 1971, reports Robert Chesshyre in the *Observer* of that month, the Gay Liberation Front had crossed the Atlantic from New York to London, and 'Gay Lib' members held meetings at universities and 'homosexual pubs', distributing magazines and pamphlets. In the year of Bowie's *Melody*

Maker interview, however, 'gay' was still being used without hesitation to mean 'happy', as in 'gay abandon' – 'Town in Gay Scoring Mood', announced a *Guardian* sports writer in October 1972, while the newspaper's country diarist described a field in May as 'gay with lambs' – or 'bright', in promotions for a 'gay PVC binder' for recipes and a casual vinyl bag in 'gay colours' (November 1972). *The Times*, similarly, discussed the 'gay colours' of a Lowry portrait (January 1972) and, in its food section, offered recipes for a 'gay party drink'. Horses on the racing form of 1972 were named 'Gay Bruce', 'Gay Crocket', 'Gay Trinket', and even simply 'Gay Guy', without any apparent nudge or wink.

On the arts pages, film reviewer Derek Malcolm praised Eric Rohmer's *Death in the Afternoon* (1972), based around a married man's affair with another woman, as a 'gay, erotic, tender and clear-sighted movie'; in *The Times*, George Steiner discussed Kierkegaard's 'gay sadness'. The other, newer meaning was certainly creeping in: a review of Robin Maugham's *Escape from the Shadows* from *The Times* of September 1972 opens bluntly with 'Lots of them these days, there are, sitting on the shelves: gay-queer-faggot-homosexual books.' But it's clear that 'gay' was still ambiguous when Bowie dropped his bombshell: in the mainstream British press at least, its primary associations were not with homosexuality at all.

We might argue that readers of the *Melody Maker* were

closer to the subculture that had, as Dyer suggests, known the other connotations of 'gay' for decades. Michael Watts's use of the Polari slang term 'varda' (also spelled 'vada') signified his insider status. But even within Bowie's circle, the word was slippery. Lead guitarist Mick Ronson, for instance, explained that 'I'm gay in as much as I wear girls' shoes and have bangles on my wrist, but I was doing that before I met David.' Having a gay image, he acknowledged, 'is the "in" thing'. In this reading, gay simply seems to signify feminine clothes and accessories, or a trendy style. Angie implied a different meaning again when she reassured Ronson's mother that 'David just chose a dramatic way of saying we think gay people are cool, that's all': his coming-out confession is rewritten here into a confirmation that he was, in our contemporary terms, an LGBT ally.

'Gay' could also, confusingly, include 'bisexual'. David was married to Angie of course, and had a son, but in 1972 being in a serious relationship with a woman would not have contradicted his claim in the *Melody Maker*. While bisexuality was becoming increasingly recognised, it tended to be included – in both popular and psychiatric discourse – within that flexible category of 'gay'; as a middle ground between heterosexual and homosexual, rather than a distinct identity of its own. It was not named on the Kinsey scale, and the first bi-specific support groups, liberation movements, magazines and academic studies were all established in or after 1972.

As Pete Shelley from the Buzzcocks confirmed:

By 1972 David Bowie came out, and I was a big Bowie fan
as well. To me that seemed right, that's who I am. The
problem with saying you were gay was that your girlfriend
used to get very confused. For many years, bisexuality
seemed to be a non-existent status. Straight people consider
you to be gay, and gay people consider you to be straight,
or gay but without any commitment.

A *Guardian* article from January of that year offers another
useful snapshot of contemporary attitudes. Former MP Ian
Harvey, who had himself been arrested for 'gross indecency'
in 1958 and been forced to resign from his ministerial post,
divided contemporary 'homosexual society' into three catego-
ries, including gay men who 'desire to change', those who
accept themselves as they are, and finally, 'those who are
bisexual and whose approach is therefore variable'. 'The condition of the bisexual,' he reported in his assessment of gay
rights since the 1967 law, 'is probably the most improved:
the fear of criminal punishment has been removed. The risk
of blackmailing has been largely eliminated.'

So, while the distinction between the 'G' and 'B' of LGBT
is clear to us now, at the moment of Bowie's *Melody Maker*
interview, bisexuality was broadly regarded as a safer, more
palatable type of gayness: as a 'fig-leaf', or, as one letter in

response to Harvey's article suggested, a 'superior' form of an unfortunate condition. Times were changing, but there was no perceived contradiction between Bowie saying he was gay or bisexual in 1972; both terms placed him firmly in the same camp. His *Melody Maker* coming-out statement, then, was far more ambiguous than it might now seem.

That Bowie's 'gay' image – 'gay' in all the early 1970s senses of the word – was partly Angie's idea adds a further complication. Her memoirs describe his androgynous style as 'a crucial factor, of inestimable value to David's career', and she claims retrospective credit for converting him from his 'hippie rut' to the man-dresses, the make-up and the orange Ziggy hair; dyed and cut by her own stylist, Suzi Fussey. Her response to the *Melody Maker* piece, according to her autobiography, is telling: 'David! You've fucking *made* it! There's gonna be no stopping us now, babe! Marketing-wise, it was just perfect.' David displayed a similar, media-savvy cynicism – after the Oxford gig where he famously sank to his knees in front of Ronson's guitar, he screamed at photographer Mick Rock, 'Did you get it, did you get it?' – but there's a strong sense that Angie pushed him towards this new, 'polysexual stardust alien' persona. 'Which of course,' she adds shrewdly, 'did the trick, imagewise.'

Mrs Ronson had phoned Haddon Hall after the *Melody Maker* interview, concerned about what her son was getting into. She had valid reasons to be worried. 'Gay' may have been a difficult word to pin down in 1972, but people didn't have to understand precisely what it meant, or what they meant by it, to know that they didn't like it. Ronson remembered that 'my family in Hull took a lot of flak about it because they'd never even heard about it up there . . . it came like throwing paint over the car and paint up the front door.' Bowie, too, faced homophobia in the United States wearing his Mr Fish dress; he was refused entry to a restaurant on his first night in LA 'on the grounds that he was a transvestite', says Nicholas Pegg, and was 'threatened by a gun-toting redneck', according to David Buckley.

Bowie's performance of 'Starman' on *Top of the Pops* in July 1972 earned a similarly hostile response, according to those who remember watching it with their parents. 'Fathers shouted "Poofter!" and "Nancy boy!" at the screen,' recalls Dylan Jones, 'and wondered why Bowie and Ronson were clinging so close to each other, why they had their arms draped around each other's shoulder so tightly. Why were they both dressed so strangely? Did they want to look like women?'

A fan called Michelle, quoted in Fred and Judy Vermorel's book *Starlust*, remembers seeing this 'colourful man, or perhaps it was a woman, I really couldn't tell . . . in the centre of her TV'. She asked her parents who it was. 'Oh . . . that's David Bowie. He's gay.'

A generation of Bowie fans was empowered by this bold

subversion, which, as we saw from the earlier testimonies, helped them to discover their own identities – but they also took the brunt of the bullying. 'Being a Bowie fan meant that your schoolmates branded you a "poof", too,' reports David Buckley. Marc Almond agrees that, after 'Starman', 'all hell broke loose in the playground. Bowie was a queer, and if you liked him you must be queer too.' Ian McCulloch was taunted on the bus: 'Eh la, have you got lippy on? Are you a boy or a girl? All my other mates at school would say, "Did you see that bloke on *Top of the Pops*? He's a right faggot, him!"'

In all these responses to the 'Starman' performance of 1972, gender non-conformity is conflated with gayness. McCulloch's schoolmates made the connection between wearing lippy, looking androgynous and being a faggot. The dads imagined by Dylan Jones wonder both why Ronson and Bowie are touching so closely, and whether they're trying to dress like women. Michelle from *Starlust* can't tell if Bowie is a boy or a girl, either: her parents simply offer 'he's gay' as an explanation.

There was, in fact, an established history of alliance between drag queens and gay men – what John Gill calls an 'interlocking hierarchy of gender and sexual identity' – most obvious during the Stonewall riots of 1969. Richard Dyer describes drag and camp as 'the most well-known and obvious aspects of traditional male culture in its showbiz inflection', and notes that the early gay liberation movement included 'unshaven men wearing frocks or men going to work wearing skimpy women's jumpers with flower motifs on them' as a gesture towards their sexual nonconformity.

But the kids on the school buses, and the dads in the living rooms, weren't necessarily aware of any 'interlocking hierarchy'. They didn't have to know exactly what 'gay' meant – whether it included bisexuality, or whether it meant wearing lipstick and dresses like a transvestite. 'Poofter', 'Nancy boy' and 'faggot' neatly encompassed all those forms of difference and deviancy: everything that wasn't straight. So to an extent, it doesn't matter exactly what Bowie meant by 'gay'. He was boldly demonstrating nonconformity in a range of ways – his public statements, his feminine outfits, his provocative physical interactions with Ronson – and whatever his motivation, he was taking genuine risks, with a genuinely subversive effect.

Was this subversion all Angie's idea, as she suggests? In a word, no. Sometimes the answer is simply no. Bowie was clearly provoking and experimenting with sexual and gender conventions long before he met Angela Barnett – his Long-Haired Men campaign and statement that he preferred boys date back to 1964 – and he'd been fascinated with costumes, masks and alternate personae for years. Recall that he'd tried to persuade The Konrads to adopt a Wild West image (1963), that he dressed them all in uniforms and then customised his own jacket for the Riot Squad (1967), where he was credited as 'Toy Soldier'; that he'd played the manifestation of a painted portrait in *The Image* (January 1969) and a mime discovering the price of fame in *The Mask* (February 1969), all before his first date with Angela in April 1969. Her hard-headed, business-minded attitude certainly shaped the 'polysexual stardust alien' image, but drag, dressing up and playful performance were in David's make-up since he tried on his mother's cosmetics at the age of three.

On one level, Bowie's public statements about bisexuality and gayness – like his visual statements, with the dresses and make-up – were part of his self-promotion; a deliberate attempt to shock the media and grab publicity. His flirtation and occasional affairs with older men in the business also seem, to an extent, like stepping stones in his relentless drive towards professional success. But he was also, as we saw in the last chapter, intrigued by the process of borrowing from diverse cultural sources, combining them in new ways, and discovering what happened when they mixed together. His claim to be bisexual was not, I'd suggest, just about marketing, or an honest expression of his own preferences, though it was both of those things. It was also a sign of his deeper and broader interest in change, and in the spaces between apparently binary points. The idea of not being entirely gay or straight, not being a man or a woman, being 'not sure if you're a boy or a girl', wearing a 'man's dress', are all connected to this fascination.

We can see it in the cover for *Hunky Dory*, where Bowie's

languid, soft-focus pose was modelled on a pin-up of Marlene Dietrich, and in the twinned, gender-switching titles 'Ziggy Stardust' and 'Lady Stardust', two tracks apart on the same album.

We can hear it in the ambiguity of 1972's 'John, I'm Only Dancing' ('she turns me on, but I'm only dancing'), and in the impatient shift of attention from men to women across Bowie's early seventies lyrics. In 'The Width of a Circle', which opens *The Man Who Sold the World*, he offers a frenzied confession about a man who 'swallowed his pride and puckered his lips, and showed me the leather belt round his hips'; by side two of the LP, on 'She Shook Me Cold', he's relating a similar passing encounter with a woman: 'She sucked my dormant will . . . mother she blew my brain.' In 'Suffragette City', the narrator boasts about his exploits with a 'mellow-thighed chick' and tells his buddy to get out, because 'there's only room for one, and here she comes, here she comes'; on 'Moonage Daydream', also on the *Ziggy Stardust* LP, he's decided that 'the church of man, love' – or perhaps 'man-love' – 'is such a holy place to be.'

That last line meant a lot to Lev Raphael, who took it as an affirmation of Bowie's gayness. But Bowie's interests and urges at the time were, I'd suggest, too complex and fluid to be pinned down by any single label, and the key to them lies in two other, less obvious lines from the same song: 'I'm a mama-papa coming for you,' and 'You're squawking like a pink monkey-bird.' Rather than being fully invested in bisexuality as an identity, Bowie enjoyed juxtaposition and in-betweenness. He liked to toy with the spaces between terms, and to join oppositional ideas into hybrid forms. On a playful level, this tendency is evident in his puns, which rely on an ambiguity between sounds and produce a new, dual meaning through the combination of words: 'Space Oddity', 'gnomad', 'Rubber Band', 'A Lad Insane'. A pun contains two ideas within a single term, much like a monkey-bird, a mama-papa – again, a merging of gender roles into a hermaphrodite figure – or, in 1974, a diamond dog.

Of course, the diamond dog isn't a combination of animal with mineral, as the name suggests: it's a canine man, appearing on the album cover as a form of sphinx, with Bowie's head and the body of a hound. Guy Peellaert's painting is based on two sets of photographs, one showing Bowie lounging on the floor, and the other with a dog in his place. The final art merges the two into a fantastic hybrid, again like a monkey-bird, or a mama-papa, or by extension a boy-girl, a man-dress, or a gay-bisexual: neither entirely one thing nor another. He liked it that way. Bowie didn't want to fly any political flags for bisexuality, or serve as a figurehead. ('I don't want to be a leader. After all, who wants to be a cause?') On one level, his public bisexuality was simply about remaining unguessable as an individual. He saw it, in keeping with the popular discourse of the time, as a fluid middle ground; a space between the binary points of 'straight' and 'gay'.

Significantly, too, he never claimed to be a woman, despite his dresses, make-up and long hair, and the confusion from TV viewers. He wanted to maintain that uncertainty, the 'not sure if you're a boy or a girl' aspect of it all. The most important thing to Bowie, during this period, was never to be still: to shift and flow between points, to keep up momentum, to resist labels and escape categorisation. As soon as he felt he'd stayed in one place for too long, he moved on. That drive motivated him, and shaped his creative work, for decades.

We can see this impetus in his relentless progress through styles and genres in the 1960s, as he discarded bands and managers in his uneven climb towards solo success; but also in his 1970s career, when he'd achieved his goal but didn't want to lose the energy. He'd sought stardom for years as a teenager, catching it briefly, only to have it snatched away. His first album had sunk. 'Space Oddity' hit, but the follow-up bombed, making him look like a one-hit wonder with a novelty song. He'd been dumped by record labels, passed over in auditions, tried out alternate careers as an actor and mime. Now he'd finally seized his moment, he wasn't going to burn out like a supernova, or soar briefly, then fade. As Cameron Crowe surmised in his 1976 article for *Playboy*: 'David Bowie, it's safe to say, would do anything to make it. And now that he has made it, he'll do anything to stay there.'

He had to keep moving. He had to keep shifting to surprise the public and maintain media attention; and he needed that public platform so he could keep producing his art, partly just to get the crazy energy out of himself and stay ahead of the family schizophrenia. 'I could put all my psychological excesses into my music and then I could be always throwing it off.' So he killed Ziggy Stardust at the height of that character's fame, and changed his name to Aladdin Sane. His elaborately theatrical *Diamond Dogs* tour mutated during its run, becoming the 'Philly Dogs' tour as Bowie impatiently adapted it to his new interest in soul music, and debuted tracks from his next album, *Young Americans*. For his next trick, he was going to become another composite: a white performer of black music, a blue-eyed soul singer.

Philosophers Delueze and Guattari, who we encountered in the previous chapter, refer to similar hybrids in their work: the 'leopard-men, crocodile-men . . . wolf-men, goat-men' of cultural ritual. This kind of becoming, they argue, is a form of multiplicity, a passage from one self to another. Each transformation takes us through a threshold. 'The only way to get outside the dualisms is to be-between, to pass between, the intermezzo . . . never ceasing to become.' It could have been Bowie's philosophy. The only way to keep moving is to keep becoming. The only way to escape binaries is to move constantly in between. The only way to avoid stagnation is to change. Keep slipping and shifting from one identity to the next. Don't let them pin you down and put you in a box. Don't let the madness catch and consume you: channel it outwards into your work.

Of course, the idea of Bowie as an artist who went through changes is nothing new; and neither is the idea of him as a cultural magpie, picking and choosing, and piecing together items he liked. But a magpie attitude implies a quick flyby, spotting shiny things, swooping down to grab them, then taking them straight back to the nest. He did better than that. Bowie was more than a casual cultural tourist: he put the work in, and genuinely immersed himself in his chosen environment. He was one of the few white people in the audiences at Harlem clubs and theatres during his immersion in mid-1970s black music, and impressed guitarist Carlos Alomar with his personal collection of vintage R&B and jazz records. Whatever his exact relationship to the gay community of the early 1970s, he was a regular at the Sombrero club, in Kensington (now a branch of Santander), and, later, a patron of the Anderes Ufer in Berlin (he once helped them fix their shop window, which had been smashed in a homophobic protest). While in Berlin, Bowie dated club manager Romy Haag, who was, in the vocabulary of the time, transsexual. He didn't just swoop in, steal and head back home: he stayed for a while and lived the lifestyle.

But then – and this is the crux – he left again. His investment was sincere and his interest genuine, but they didn't last: they couldn't last. He had to keep up that nomadic momentum, as he confessed in a reflective, self-aware lyric from *Lodger*, towards the end of the decade: 'Sometimes I feel that I need to move on. So I pack a bag . . . and I move on.' As simple as that. He was a superstar, and the ability to escape was one of his privileges. 'Well, I might take a train, or sail at dawn . . .' He had those options. He could embrace a culture, its music and its styles, then change cities and adopt a new persona, a new direction for a new album: a new career in a new town. Black musicians in Harlem did not have those options. The ordinary patrons of the Sombrero and the Anderes Ufer didn't have those options. 'Might take a girl . . . when I move on.' The song casts Bowie as a wandering playboy. Its melody, significantly, is the glam anthem 'All the Young Dudes', played backwards. He was revising and reversing his earlier position, preparing to leave the seventies behind.

Bowie could playfully say he was gay, straight or bisexual, and ride out the consequences; he could pose as an androgynous alien, then kill that character and tell everyone to call him the Thin White Duke. He could become a blue-eyed soul singer, recruiting the best musicians from that scene and recording at their favourite studio, then dump the band, cross the world and produce art rock. His real self was deeply hidden. None of his fans truly knew him. He could pick up identities, then shed them. He treated bisexuality like a hairstyle, and black culture like folk music, mod or glam;

they worked for a while, but could be cut and dropped when they'd served their purpose. (He did the same with people – many of his collaborators report that he cut contact once a particular phase in his life was over.) He could look back on the early 1970s from a perspective in 1983, and laugh ruefully at his youthful mistakes, from the garish outfits to the unfortunate public statements. 'The past, of course, plagues him,' writes journalist Kurt Loder in *Rolling Stone*. This was Bowie's second most infamous interview, and the title is telling: 'Straight Time'. 'All those masks he no longer needs, the old poses – they keep popping up anew. "The biggest mistake I ever made," he said one night after a couple of cans of Foster's lager, "was telling that *Melody Maker* writer that I was bisexual. Christ, I was so *young* then. I was *experimenting*."'

All those masks, all those poses; all those voices and styles in the imaginary museum. A key complaint about postmodernist art is that it remains superficial in its sampling, quoting and recycling, and lacks any political awareness. Bowie's dressing up in cultural costumes, despite its sincere intentions, had the same problem. His ice-cold Thin White Duke, modelled partly on the Emcee from Kander and Ebb's musical *Cabaret* – which was based, in turn, on Christopher Isherwood's account of 1930s Berlin – came with remarks that 'Britain could benefit from a fascist leader,' and waves to the waiting crowd that looked worryingly like a Nazi salute.

'I'd adore to be prime minister,' he told Cameron Crowe for *Rolling Stone* in February 1976. 'And I believe very strongly in fascism.' As Paul Trynka suggests, 'while not a racist, David was happy to flirt with fascistic imagery in search of a newspaper headline.' The focus had changed since 1972, but the provocative baiting was very similar: 'I think I might have been a bloody good Hitler,' was Bowie's new 'I'm gay, and always have been,' updated for the mid-seventies. Tellingly, his subsequent *Playboy* interview with Crowe, from September 1976, rewrites the 1972 exchange with Michael Watts from *Melody Maker*, as if assuming that nobody would ever check the original; and rearranges the history of gay liberation around himself for good measure.

Someone asked me in an interview once – I believe it was in '71 – if I were gay. I said, 'No, I'm bisexual. The guy, a writer for one of the English trades, had no idea what the term meant. So I explained it to him. It was all printed – and that's where it started. It's so nostalgic now, isn't it? . . . Everybody wanted to see the freak. But they were so ignorant about what I was doing. There was very little talk of bisexuality or gay power before I came along. Unwittingly, I really brought that thing over . . . it took a bit of exposure and a few heavy rumours about me before the gays said, 'We disown David Bowie.' And they did. Of course. They knew that I wasn't what they were fighting for. Nobody understood the European way of dressing and adopting the asexual, androgynous everyman pose. People all went screaming, 'He's got make-up on and he's wearing stuff that looks like dresses!'

Bowie casually – and perhaps deliberately – revises the past so much that the details of what he actually said and did, and at what point, become blurred. By this point, though, his stance towards bisexuality had also changed, and become more openly cynical. 'It's true,' he told Crowe. 'I am a bisexual. But I can't deny that I've used that fact very well . . . girls are always presuming that I've kept my heterosexual virginity for some reason. So I've had all these girls try to get me over to the other side again: "C'mon, David, it isn't all that bad. I'll show you." Or, better yet, "We'll show you." I always play dumb.'

Bisexuality was, he now admitted – at least in part – a means to an end. He was entirely willing to pretend he'd had no sexual experience with women, in order to gain even more sexual experience with women: to that extent, his 'gayness' was a performance and pose. To him, no doubt, the aspiration to be Hitler was also a pose, a throwaway remark in exactly the same vein as his boast, earlier in the interview, that 'I want to be a Frank Sinatra figure. And I will succeed.' Bowie's error, of course, was not realising that poses, masks and costumes carry serious cultural weight, as well as more superficial connotations, and that he couldn't just cut them away from those frameworks: they had broader meaning beyond his own personal dressing-up box. Claiming to be gay was a neat way of grabbing attention and keeping people guessing, but it also, despite his protests that he didn't want to be a Gay Lib leader – although ironically, he was happy enough to put himself forward as a fascist Prime Minister a few years later – made him an icon to marginalised fans. When he picked up and dropped gayness and bisexuality, he picked up and dropped those people, too. He changed for his own personal and professional reasons, and it kept him dynamic and vibrant – he might have even said it kept him alive. But when he changed as an individual, he left others behind; and, as we saw, they sometimes felt betrayed.

Bowie's more overtly political songs have, perhaps unsurprisingly in this context, never been his most successful. 'China Girl', despite Bowie's stated intention to parody racist attitudes, and its lyrical suggestions of colonialism ('I'll give you television . . . I'll give you the man who wants to rule the world'), plays as an uncritical series of 'Oriental' stereotypes. His attempts at topical 'protest' songs with Tin Machine – 'Crack City', 'I Can't Read', 'Video Crime' – were often crassly obvious. Precise and deft in so many respects, he was clumsy in his grasp on broader issues of cultural power and oppression, or at least in his expression of that understanding through his music: 'Valentine's Day', towards the end of his career, is a subtler exception, with its discreet references to gun violence.

But Bowie's 1983 renunciation of his bisexuality was politically shrewd. It was political in the way he understood best – on the personal level, in terms of how changing trends related to himself and his own career. It was as canny as his claim to be bisexual had been, eleven years before; it was a clever adaptation of his brand image, for a very different moment. In 1972, as we saw, 'gay' had multiple meanings. By the mid-eighties it had acquired a new one, as Colin Clews demonstrates in *Gay in the 80s: From Fighting for Our Rights to Fighting for Our Lives*. The British tabloids were rife with stories about the 'Gay Plague' or, less commonly, the 'Gay Bug'. 'AIDS is the Wrath of God, says Vicar', reported *The Sun* newspaper in February 1985. 'A Million Will Have AIDS in Six Years', warned the *Daily Mail*. *The Sun*, again, reported on social policing and protection from this 'plague', offering examples for others to follow: 'BANNED! AIDS-fear Club Ousts Gay Couple', 'Pub Ban on Gays in AIDS Panic'. In terms of career preservation, Bowie had judged the mood perfectly. For his gay fans, though, it was cruel timing.

Mitchell Plitnick's article 'We Can Be Heroes' describes the context of the 1983 *Rolling Stone* interview.

It wasn't only Bowie. In 1983, AIDS was really making its way into the headlines and hatred of gay men was rampant. Much of the progress that had been made since the 1960s' gay liberation movement was being reversed. The gay culture that was so open during the Decade of Disco was being forced back underground under the cloud of a devastating epidemic. Worse for me, bisexual men were seen as the 'conduit' the 'gay disease' was using to infect heterosexuals.

Ironically, of course, Bowie – whatever his intentions at the time – had helped to further that cause during the 1970s, by inspiring individuals and challenging conventions. As David Buckley writes: 'for those unsure about their sexuality or who were in agonies about "coming out", Bowie at least let them know that someone (and someone talented and cool to boot) was listening.' Mitchell Plitnick again offers a personal example: knowing he was bisexual from an early age, he grappled with 'shame, denial and an overwhelming fear of discovery. But Bowie put another feeling inside me, one of pride and a sense that this brilliant artist was just like me, at least in one way.'

As we saw earlier, Plitnick heard lines like 'the church of man, love, is such a holy place to be' as an affirmation. In 1983 those explicit references to gay culture and identity were replaced by a cautious cover of 'Criminal World', originally recorded by Metro in 1977. Bowie erases two lines that, again ironically, were no doubt inspired by songs like 'Queen Bitch', and replaces them with vaguer, safer lyrics. 'I'm not the queen so there's no need to bow . . . I'll take your dress and we can truck on out,' sings Peter Godwin in the 1977 version. Bowie switches it to 'I guess I recognise your destination . . . what you want is sort of separation.' Chris O'Leary calls this tamer cover 'a mistake, an insult, one of his least noble moments'.

In 1993 Bowie doubled down on his previous statements, again in *Rolling Stone*:

> I think I was always a closet heterosexual. I didn't ever feel that I was a real bisexual. It was like I was making all the moves, down to the situation of actually trying it out with some guys . . . I wanted to imbue Ziggy with real flesh and blood and muscle, and it was imperative that I find Ziggy and be him. The irony of it was that I was not gay. I was physical about it, but frankly it wasn't enjoyable. It was almost like I was testing myself. It wasn't something I was comfortable with at all. But it had to be done.

This was a new revision of his past, over twenty years since the *Melody Maker* interview: and perhaps it came closer to the truth. His investment in gay and bisexual culture was, according to this account, a kind of method acting, similar to dressing up in Warhol's clothes for *Basquiat*. It was sincerely meant, but it was still a performance.

As he approached his fiftieth birthday, Bowie enjoyed a last burst of pantomime daftness, dressing up like a punk uncle in his distressed designer clothes by McQueen, with spiked orange hair and dark eye make-up. 'Do you like girls or boys?' he wondered in 'Hallo Spaceboy' (1995), echoing the gender subversion of 'Rebel Rebel', but adopting an ironic, older-generation perspective. 'It's confusing these days.'

By the end of the century, however, he'd entered a calmer, more contemplative and mature phase. On *Earthling* he'd tried to chase the current moment, incorporating drum 'n' bass to mixed critical responses. On *'hours...'*, he played the role of a curator, looking back down the years. The opening track, 'Thursday's Child', begins, 'All of my life I've tried so hard, doing my best with what I had.' In the video, Bowie gazes into a mirror and sees his younger self. Of course, he's playing a character again – he wasn't even born on a Thursday – but it's notable that in this portrayal of his quieter, meditative moments, both the older and younger Bowie figures have a woman at their side.

There was one more public statement about his sexuality, made early in the next decade: he was almost making it an anniversary event. This conversation was with *Blender* magazine in 2002, and Bowie was answering questions from fans.

We have someone who called himself 'Whoodaamann', from Arizona, to thank for bringing it up again. 'You once said that saying you were bisexual was "the biggest mistake I ever made". Do you still believe that?'

'Interesting,' muses Bowie, and the interviewer, Clark Collis, records a 'long pause' before he replies.

> I don't think it was a mistake in Europe, but it was a lot tougher in America. I had no problem with people knowing I was bisexual. But I had no inclination to hold any banners or be a representative of any group of people. I knew what I wanted to be, which was a songwriter and a performer, and I felt that [bisexuality] became my headline over here for so long. America is a very puritanical place, and I think it stood in the way of so much I wanted to do.

In this final revision, Bowie's bisexuality becomes, once again, a genuine part of his identity, and his denial of it is reiterated as a pragmatic decision. Interestingly, this reminiscence, three decades later, echoes some of Bowie's key statements from the 1970s: that he didn't want to carry a flag for any campaigns, and, as he suggested in 1976, that his European approach didn't play so well in the very different cultural climate of the US. He'd learned that lesson early, when a redneck pulled a gun on him in his Mr Fish dress.

His words ring true here, because they tally with the

overriding, driving impulse I mentioned before. He had to keep making his art, above all – getting that energy out of his system – and to do that, he had to keep changing, and moving forward. That was the priority. He had to keep creating, and he couldn't let anything hold him back. If bisexuality became a barrier, it would have to be dropped – with the same brutal logic that had led him, far earlier in his career, to ditch his teenage bands, turn his back on folk music and kill his first stage persona.

His motives, if we trust him at this point, are understandable on a personal and professional level. He was selfishly thinking of himself rather than the broader cultural impact; on the other hand, he felt that retaining the bisexual associations would have killed his career by 1983, which of course would have deprived the world of every album after *Scary Monsters*. But where did this leave the fans who had felt betrayed? An article in *Slate*, from 2016, suggested one way of negotiating the uneven and uncertain landscape of Bowie's sexuality.

Now that the man behind Ziggy is also dead, we for whom queerness is not a phase seem to have two options in terms of how we deal with Bowie's fraught relationship to our name and our stuff. We can be pissed off and view his career as, at least in part, an act of sly cultural appropriation – one of many that pop has committed at our expense over the years. Or, more generously, we can allow that even if Bowie was not really sexually queer (gay, bi, or otherwise), he was one of the most culturally queer artists to grace this earth.

Or, as a *New York Times* headline put it on 13 January 2016: 'Was He Gay, Bisexual or Bowie? Yes'. Bowie was being afforded his own unique, individual type of queerness, and it was in this generous, grateful context, just after his passing, that a 'closet heterosexual' who'd openly said he never wanted to lead a liberation campaign was celebrated as the figurehead of a genderqueer movement: a movement that had never been dreamed of in 1970, when Bowie first lounged, long-haired, in his man's dress.

What can we learn from this history? On one level, it's healthy to acknowledge that our heroes are always 'heroes'; that Bowie was flawed and made mistakes. His oversight, in this case, was to ignore the political consequences of his personal choices. We can understand that he needed to cut and run, and constantly move on throughout the 1970s, in order to keep up his creative momentum. We can understand why he felt the need to ditch his image from the early 1970s in order to relaunch himself for mainstream America in 1983. He could see the future coming, and he adapted to it. But in his urgent energy of the 1970s he tended to be selfish; and in the early 1980s he was career-minded and pragmatic to a fault. He adopted communities and cultures, then left them behind when their time, for him, had passed. They continued, of course, without him, but they felt the sting of his departure.

If we do choose to forgive Bowie, as *Slate* writer J. Bryan Lowder suggested, and see him as 'culturally queer', is it also appropriate to herald him, in retrospect, as the pioneer of a non-binary movement? As we saw, he resisted any leadership roles, and the words themselves would have been unfamiliar during the early 1970s, when Bowie was at his most androgynous. In strictly historical terms, to apply current vocabulary back to a different cultural moment is to impose our own values and understanding on the past, and it should be done cautiously, with provisos: Romy Haag might now identify as transgender, for instance, but the word was simply not available for her to use at the time.

On our own personal levels though, as I've suggested, Bowie belongs to each of us individually, and the meanings he offers us are outside history. It would be hypocritical of anyone who has integrated Bowie into their life, been inspired and influenced by him, and merged his matrix with their own, to try to control, contain or deny the readings that other people draw from his work. Dylan Jones recalls of the early-seventies Bowie that 'I preferred evidence that my bisexual hero was more straight than gay,' for example. 'So it was good news he was married to Angie, less good they'd reportedly first met when sleeping with the same guy'; the album cover for *The Man Who Sold the World*, liberating and affirming to some, made him 'uncomfortable'. We may not share his experience, but his interpretation is valid and significant. This is how Dylan Jones negotiated David Bowie's image and behaviour in 1970, when Jones was ten years old, and no doubt many other ten-year-old boys felt similarly at the time.

I mentioned in the introduction the way David Bowie made me feel when I was thirteen, in 1983. My own response to the *Let's Dance* album and its hit songs was quite different from the way this period in Bowie's career is remembered by biographers and critics; as a turn towards the mainstream, a disavowal of earlier subversion, and a betrayal of his gay fans.

I watched the video for 'Let's Dance' many times in the mid-eighties, after taping it from the *Max Headroom* show. I didn't see Bowie as a confident, cynical businessman. I saw him as slight and fragile, backed up against the wall of a rough Australian pub, his expression strained, and I connected with how he must feel in that situation. Bowie, his hair in a bleached, teased quiff, is the only one in formal clothes – a shirt, waistcoat and matching white gloves and shoes – and he seems entirely out of place. There's a distance across the tiled floor between him and the locals, who glare and laugh at him in reaction shots. An older guy in shorts gets off his chair and does a mocking, chicken-armed dance to the beat, while his friends grin. Bowie isn't looking at the locals. He glances to one side, his lip curled. He seems to squint and grimace as he sings, isolated but defiant. He's not a star entertainer with an appreciative crowd. He's performing despite the fact that he's unwelcome and outnumbered.

Of course, there are other ways to read the video. 'Let's Dance' is most obviously about race, and we could note the contrast between Bowie and the locals, on one hand, and the fluid, easy dancing of the two Aboriginal performers, Joelene King and Terry Roberts. We could easily adopt a class-based analysis, noting that Bowie descended on a genuine pub, the Carinda Hotel, and took it over for his shoot, making working Australians into his supporting cast. Journalist Dean Goodman reports that 'as the beer flowed freely, courtesy of Bowie, the staunch ranchers ridiculed the gloved Pommie bastard at every opportunity – as can be seen in the video. Bowie, in turn, called them rednecks.'

But I saw the video – though I wouldn't have been able to articulate it in this way at the time, and wouldn't have acknowledged it to myself – as about sexuality. Unaware of the surrounding discourse and the 'Straight Time' interview – I was more likely to read the *Radio Times* than *Rolling Stone* when I was thirteen – I felt something for Bowie that was partly attraction, partly identification and partly aspiration. As a slight, well-behaved boy at a rough school, I connected with the sensation of being cornered in a tough, hostile space, and in Bowie's squints and grimaces I saw a kind of conflict, as if he were trying to contain something that wanted to escape, or communicate something he was holding back. Perhaps on a semi-conscious level, I related his position in the bar to the phrase people used at school in response to any hint of gayness: 'backs to the walls, lads!' I saw something of myself in him, and I wanted to be more like him: beautiful and brave.

I wasn't gay. But it didn't matter at school in the mid-eighties. If you didn't mess about enough in class, you were gay. If you wore anything outside the approved fashions, you were gay. If you didn't conform to a narrow type of masculinity, you were gay. So for various reasons, I was called a poofter, a bum-bandit and a gender-bender, and was punished accordingly. I was interested in girls, but my fascination with Bowie – and, in turn, with the two gorgeous guys from Go West, whose poster was above my bed – inclined me to think that I could be what people said, or something similar. By the time I entered sixth form, I'd found the confidence to turn it back on people. One boy slipped me a note that read: 'You gay bastard.' I wrote a short poem back to him: 'I opened your letter, and it made me cry. For I am not gay, though I might just be bi.' He told me he didn't like the sentiment of my reply, but he begrudgingly admired the skill.

From the point of view of my sixteen-year-old self, then, I can appreciate what Bowie was trying to do with his 1970s interviews. He was gaining and maintaining media attention, certainly, to push his own brand, but he was also provoking and subverting; and despite his disclaimers about not wanting to lead a movement, that subversion was political. His embracing of bisexuality was a form of positive representation. I knew I was doing something similar, on a very small scale, when I responded to accusations of being gay, in the mid-eighties, by openly accepting the possibility rather than denying it. I wanted to empty the word of insult, and turn it around into a kind of compliment.

I wasn't gay. I was something else that I didn't have words for; the words barely existed even in the broader adult culture of the time. I'd been a pretty child, with longish blond hair, and I always remembered the occasions when I was mistaken for a girl. I liked that idea of fluidity, and when I was ten I had a fantasy that the control on my Pong console, which could flip from 'TV' to 'Game', might also work in the same way on me, switching from male to female. I didn't tell anyone, and if I had, it would have seemed like typical make-believe. But if a ten-year-old made that announcement now, we might identify them as transgender. Times change, and terms change, and our lives are shaped by those shifting cultural frameworks.

I never fully lost my childhood love of dressing up. But I realised, of course, that while a little boy could happily wear a clown outfit or soldier uniform to nursery school, a teenage boy who liked costume jewellery and make-up, as I did, had to keep it very quiet. In my early twenties, living on my own and mixing in what we would now call queer social circles, I was able to indulge those tastes much more. I ran a fanzine about 'comics, cosmetics and crossdressing', with a male and female editor. Both of them were me. It would be neat to say that Bowie was my soundtrack to those years, but his period as the bearded leader of a four-man band in Tin Machine, and the subsequent *Black Tie White Noise*, celebrating his marriage to Iman, didn't speak to me at the time. I found more connection in the younger bands inspired by Bowie: particularly Suede, with lyrics like 'this skinny boy's one of the girls'. Later, Placebo's 'Nancy Boy' – 'does his make-up in his room, douse himself with cheap perfume' – seemed like an entry from my own diary.

I went to Pride with gay, bisexual and lesbian friends, but there was no real community at the time for people who felt the way I did. There were pamphlets that you could send away for, and magazines in brown envelopes, and secret clubs where you could dress up and mix with people like yourself, but there was no movement or campaign. There was a limited vocabulary, and there were very few role models. I knew of Eddie Izzard, who called himself a transvestite, and Jame Gumb from *Silence of the Lambs*, who was a transsexual. It was generally assumed that the first led to the second, if you were serious and committed enough. I didn't go that way of course, although I sometimes told people I was considering it; partly to challenge them, and partly to test myself, to see if it was true.

As I described in the last chapter, I also sold out to an extent, through a sense of necessity – and so again I understand Bowie's decision in 1983, and this perhaps helps to explain why I saw so much repression and tension in his work of the time. I don't believe anyone can entirely shed a part of themselves so quickly, just because it's safer in the current climate, and I felt his old energy trying to escape through his gritted teeth in the videos for 'Let's Dance' and 'Loving the Alien'. My own past also returned, much later, prompted by the Channel 4 TV show *My Transsexual Summer* in 2011. It reminded me vividly of how I used to feel, and I recognised myself in the women on-screen.

The meaning of words shifts very quickly these days, and 'transsexual' was soon replaced by 'transgender' as the more acceptable term. Times had changed a great deal since the early 1990s. When I expressed my thoughts about gender to close friends in the early 2010s, they were immediately accepting. They would treat me as a woman, they said. I began to wear make-up again, socially, away from work, and to feel freer in how I dressed. I bought heels and had a skirt custom-made. There were campaigns now, and communities, and I would have been welcomed.

It could have gone further in that direction for me. The

reason it didn't is political. Though my friends were very generous, I simply didn't feel comfortable, having enjoyed the privileged position of passing through the world as a male for decades, being accepted into what I saw as an oppressed group. I didn't feel I deserved to be treated as female, even part-time, because I hadn't earned it. I hadn't grown up that way. Yes, I'd been called a poof and a gender-bender – which, with hindsight, was the most accurate term – and I'd felt confused, taken risks and kept secrets, and wanted to be something different. But I'd nevertheless benefited all my life from being a man, just as I had by being white. Years later, in a climate of increased social acceptance, I didn't feel I had the right to flip the switch I'd toyed with when I was ten.

And this is one reason why, on a personal level, I value Bowie as someone who did everything he did – who wore dresses, heels and make-up – as a man. To argue that because he subverted gender roles he must be non-binary, seems to suggest that men cannot adopt 'feminine' styles without becoming something other-than-male; it reduces the potential for men to challenge and undermine stereotypes and conventions, while also acknowledging their maleness and all the privilege that comes with it.

The point of this story is that times change, and terms change, and that people change too, especially over a period of thirty years or more. We try to articulate our feelings through the words available to us. Sometimes we say things to provoke a reaction, and sometimes to test their truth. On my own, personal level, I was as inconsistent as Bowie – or, to be more generous, as fluid. We should, I think, allow people to evolve throughout their lives, and to bear in mind that they are expressing themselves using the vocabulary of their cultural moment; but as I've noted, we should also consider that personal choices have political consequences, especially for people with a platform like Bowie's.

I'm fully aware that I could have made different decisions at different points, and so I can understand those who took other routes from a similar position. The representation of transgender women and men – and those who identify as non-binary – within popular media is gradually improving and increasing, and this is important. But I also think it is important for us to have cultural icons, like Bowie, who challenge gender roles and presentation while remaining rooted within their birth sex. I'd suggest that men and boys, in particular, need role models who expand the possibilities of what it means to be male, without escaping it and positioning themselves within another, non-male category.

These days the term that might be applied to me is 'gender-non-conforming' male, or GNC male, which is an unwieldy and unlovely phrase, without the punch of 'genderqueer', but perhaps the most accurate: and perhaps the most accurate description of Bowie, too, for the moment. If I was ever challenged now for wearing eyeshadow and nail vanish, and feeling outnumbered or overpowered, I could make the excuse that I'm a Bowie fan researching books about him, and people would be appeased. It worked in 2015 when a beefy guy faced off with me in Hastings, where I was parading in Pierrot make-up: he called me an obscenity, then grinned and shook my hand. In fact, it's not because of Bowie: it's because of who I am, and who I've been, on and off, since I was a child. But Bowie, as in so much, provides me with the example and the role model, and the confidence to keep doing it. If someone else reads him differently, as an example of someone who stepped successfully outside gender – and if this interpretation supports and inspires them – then I think we should both allow each other our slightly different versions of the same icon. Even after his death, Bowie can change and adapt himself to fit our lives where and when we need him.

Finally, though, gender is also a word with multiple meanings. To some, it is an internal knowledge about whether they are male or female, or neither. To others, 'gender' refers to a power structure, a social hierarchy that, historically, has always privileged men and oppressed women. In this second sense, despite his challenges to the conventions of traditional male appearance and behaviour, Bowie, at least in the early seventies, falls far short.

According to Angie's memoirs, he would behave like a helpless child, complaining about being 'dreadfully sick' and needing her to fuss over him. When he toured the US, she 'spent most of that month . . . up a ladder with a paintbrush, secretly preparing our palace for its returning king'. When he got up at noon every day, she would 'squeeze him his orange juice and make a fresh pot of coffee and point him in the day's direction'. When they discussed having children, he commented 'that's a lot of work', and only agreed to the idea once she promised they would hire a nanny. When she took a brief holiday after a traumatic childbirth and postnatal depression, he was 'appalled by what I'd done'. When he failed to wash regularly, she 'simply drew a bath for him every morning and took him by the hand and led him to it. Which was fine with him; David loved being taken care of.'

We should treat Angie's account with caution, just as we do with David's, but if even half of this is true, the Bowie of Haddon Hall, in the late 1960s and early 1970s, acted like a spoiled little boy, expecting his wife to care for him as a surrogate mother. While he was publicly challenging gender conventions through his hair, clothes, make-up and perform-ance, his behaviour in private seemed to hark backwards to a reactionary past, rather than into the progressive future. It's a useful reminder that while we can still aspire to be more like Bowie, we can also, in some respects, try to be better.

4

PASSING

Then one day, everything changed.

As a Bowie fan, you still remember that day; that terrible moment when the world seemed to shift onto a different timeline. The phone call in the middle of the night, or the text – or the multiple texts, pinging in one after the other – and then the disbelieving fumble for the nearest news site to confirm. Bowie's lyrics often caption my life, and at that moment, when the truth was still held in limbo, a line from 'Ashes to Ashes' echoed urgently but uselessly in my head: 'Oh no, don't say it's true.' A tweet from Duncan Jones, as if in response. 'Very sad and sorry to say it's true.' Perhaps you still remember who first told you, and what they said, and how gently and kindly they said it, knowing how hard it would hit you. Personally, I've tried to forget the details. They're painful, even now.

I took a number of calls that morning from journalists. My distant connection to Bowie – my attempt to catch some of the light from his star – made me mildly newsworthy. I did one phone interview, realised it made me feel sadder, flatter and emptier, and refused all the others until evening. I posted a single tweet, 'David Bowie will never die,' which was favourited many times. Then I lay on my bed reading books about race and representation, trying to distract myself with academic research. Hours later, a car picked me up and took me to the BBC, where I was interviewed with Geoffrey Marsh, the co-curator of the *David Bowie Is* exhibition, and Julien Temple, who directed *Jazzin' for Blue Jean* in 1984. Afterwards, I lingered outside with Temple, neither of us wanting to go straight home. We went to a nearby pub with a dripping ceiling. He told me he'd been with Bowie when the news broke that Terry had died, in 1985. Bowie had taken Temple on a bender in Soho, a tour of dive bars and one-room drinking holes in the red light district. Bowie had ended up hiding under a bed. We didn't do that. We had a pint and shook hands, or perhaps half-hugged, and the BBC cars picked us up to take us home. Above our heads, a message in white lights circled the BT Tower, broadcasting a goodbye to David Bowie.

Everything changed. On its November release, the 'Blackstar' promo was reviewed with amused fascination and frustration: 'wonderfully odd and expansive', as Ryan Dombal wrote in *Pitchfork*. 'The "Blackstar" video begins with an eclipsed sun looking down on a woman with a tail and a bejeweled astronaut skull – and it only gets stranger from there.' Andrew Pulver, in the *Guardian*, warned that the video – directed by Johan Renck with creative guidance from Bowie, and almost ten minutes long – was at risk of becoming 'furiously self-indulgent'. 'By the time the scarecrows writhing on crucifixes show up, about two-thirds of the way through, you can tell the well of imagery is beginning to run dry: there's only so much surrealism you can throw at a wall before coherence starts to disintegrate.' Pulver found echoes and cross-references in the visuals, but his comparisons were light-hearted and superficial: the opening scene on an asteroid reminded him of *Armageddon*; Bowie's button-eyed, bandaged face recalled Neil Gaiman's *Coraline*; and he puzzled over 'the Anne Hathaway lookalike with an Angelina Ballerina mouse tail'. 'Essentially,' he concluded, 'this is a straightforward example of a surreal dream-logic film that tries to sustain itself a bit too long.'

The follow-up, 'Lazarus', earned a similar reception. 'At the risk of doing his earnest artistry a disservice,' proclaimed Harriet Gibsone on 7 January 2016, 'Hooray! Button-Eyed Bandage Boy Bowie is back!' She read the video's cultural references as

'Narnia via Nosferatu'. Sam Richards, in the *New Musical Express*, stated confidently on 8 January that the song was 'sung from the perspective of Newton', the homesick alien Bowie played in 1976 film *The Man Who Fell to Earth*. Andy Greene had reviewed it late in 2015 for *Rolling Stone*, and explained, with equal confidence, that the song was 'told from the perspective of a formerly wealthy, lost man living in New York that yearns to fly away'. Their disagreements didn't matter. It was just a music video: a typically artistic, arguably self-indulgent offering from David Bowie, who was showing new creative promise as he (incredibly) approached the end of his sixties and the start of his seventh decade in the business. Interpreting it was the usual intellectual game: a short-term one for critics, who could file their brief reviews and move on to the next release, and a longer exercise for fans to puzzle over.

After that day, of course, everything changed. The playfully enigmatic messages of 'Blackstar' and 'Lazarus' (and *Blackstar* the album, and *Lazarus* the musical) suddenly became a farewell note to be decoded and translated. The meanings were no longer frivolous but deadly serious. On 11 January the *Guardian*, which had irreverently welcomed back 'Button-Eyed Bandage Boy' four days previously, wondered: 'Was David Bowie Saying Goodbye on *Blackstar*?'. The *NME* was less tentative: 'How David Bowie Told Us He Was Dying in the "Blackstar" Video'. The imagery acquired new resonance. Instead of a nostalgic reference to Narnia, the wardrobe from

'Lazarus' now struck the *NME*'s Leonie Cooper as 'a fitting kind of coffin for an icon of style and fashion'; while the song's lyrics now immediately revealed their hidden meaning. Tim Jonze revisited 'Lazarus' for the *Guardian*: 'in the wake of the sad news, it seems to be another explicit farewell song: "Look up here," he begins, "I'm in heaven." What a staggering first line for someone who knew their time was coming to an end to write: to know that he would soon be singing it to his fans from beyond the grave.'

Leonie Cooper agreed: 'His first words "look up here, I'm in heaven / I've got scars that can't be seen" are now obviously an admission of his ill health, rather than just a fantastical musing on mortality.' Tony Visconti's public statement that 'he made *Blackstar* for us, his parting gift' authorised this new reading – he was not just Bowie's old friend, but the album's producer – and it quickly dominated reviews. 'A still living David Bowie had managed to conjure up the sound that is through the corridor to death's door,' mused Dustin Ragucos for *Popmatters*, on 12 January. 'This song becomes the episode before the series finale.' 'Becomes' is the key word here. In Bowie's posthumous conjuring trick, his last album and its singles were transformed overnight.

Though the reviews from before his death may now seem naïve, critics can hardly be blamed for their readings. They assumed that, as usual, he was writing in character; Bowie was, after all, intensely private, hiding himself behind multiple masks and fronts, and his lyrics have very rarely been auto-biographical (remember 'Thursday's Child', for instance). It was in this context that Sam Richards told his readers that 'Lazarus' was from Thomas Newton's perspective, while Andy Greene saw it as a sketch of a down-on-his-luck New Yorker. Ryan Dombal, similarly, guessed that 'Blackstar' voiced the viewpoint of 'a messianic figure whose intentions are certainly questionable and probably destructive. "You're a flash in the pan / I'm the great I Am," Bowie sings in character, poking fun at our need to explain the inexplicable while remaining as perplexing and powerful as ever.'

In fact, the reviews from late 2015 and early 2016, before that turning point on 10 January, are far more diverse in their interpretations, and embrace a range of possibilities. Posthumous theories about the meaning of 'Blackstar' and 'Lazarus' are varied in their detail, but all take as a starting point the assumption that Bowie was crafting a goodbye gift for his listeners, knowing he'd soon be gone, and speaking, for once, as himself. Ironically, the death of David Bowie overturned the 'Death of the Author' approach in this case, and returned reviewers to the position of seeing an artwork not, in Barthes's words, as 'a space of many dimensions' but 'a line of words, releasing a single "theological" meaning (the "message" of the Author-God)'. It now became a question of getting it right, and wondering how the clues had been missed.

But the process of interpretation is rarely so simple. Bowie's death, and Visconti's explanation, made it tempting to narrow down all meaning to a single, isolated message, but his final work still operated within the context of the vast, complex, shifting matrix of meaning I discussed in previous chapters. Music journalist Kitty Empire noted that she'd recognised all the hints of death and mortality when she first heard a preview of the album, and regretted not including them in her review. 'Who doesn't want to look like a seer?' But 'I recoiled from writing about what now are obvious references to dying and finality, because I was keen to avoid cliché, and ageism, and the ghastly literalism common to more confessional singer-songwriters . . . with Bowie, the starting point for analysis has never been lived experience.'

She might also have observed that these references were hardly new in Bowie's work. As academic Tanja Stark discusses in her essay 'Confronting Bowie's Mysterious Corpses', we can trace them back to 'Please Mr Gravedigger', when he was just twenty years old, and follow the theme into the 1970s through 'Rock 'n' Roll Suicide' (1972) to the 'genocide' that opens *Diamond Dogs*; closely followed, of course, by 'We Are the Dead' and 'The Chant of the Ever Circling Skeletal Family'. 'Jump They Say', from 1993, revisits suicide; *1. Outside* is a story of 'art murder'; and 'Valentine's Day' deals with a school shooting. Even during his most ostensibly upbeat, mainstream phase, Bowie announces, in the middle of 'Modern Love', that 'there's no sign of life'.

Nicholas Pegg points out, in turn, that Bowie has explored getting old since 'Cygnet Committee', written at the age of twenty-two. Though he promised he would 'Never Get Old' in 2003 – the exact phrase recurs in both 'Fantastic Voyage' and 'Buddha of Suburbia' – 'the dread of encroaching age hangs weightily over countless songs': 'consider "Changes" ("pretty soon now you're gonna get older"), "The Pretty Things Are Going to Hell" ("I find you out before you grow old"), "Cygnet Committee" ("the thinker sits alone, growing older"), "The Hearts Filthy Lesson "I'm already five years older") and "Time" ("goddamn, you're looking old"), to name but a few.'

Philosopher Simon Critchley further proposes that the 'experience of nothing' lies at the core of Bowie's music, and that his personae conceal 'our fearful sickness unto death'. He adds further motifs of mortality to Stark's already extensive list: 'Space Oddity', to him, describes 'a successful suicide attempt', while 'Oh! You Pretty Things' suggests that 'the earth is a dying dog', and 'Sunday', from *Heathen*, sounds like 'a lamentation, a prayer or a psalm for the dead'. These core themes of age and ending – in Stark's words, an 'ongoing fascination with . . . the extinguishment of life . . . a lifetime of deathly intrigue' – date back almost fifty years, to 1967. The clues were there in 'Lazarus' and 'Blackstar', sure, but they were also there in a score of other songs, and they'd never before indicated that Bowie was terminally ill.

Even on his previous album from 2013, he'd mournfully described 'walking the dead' around the Berlin of his youth, asking, 'Where Are We Now?'. As Chris O'Leary suggests, it was 'as if he was dictating a will. Final curtain stuff'; but the 'fragility of his voice was an old trick'. Bowie was just putting on the old-man pose for his surprise comeback single. On the follow-up, 'The Stars (Are Out Tonight)', he'd abandoned that elegiac delivery for a vigorous rock vocal, and a video featuring both a satirical version of himself as part of a settled, middle-aged couple (with Tilda Swinton), and a far younger, androgynous incarnation, played by Iselin Steiro. 'Where Are We Now?' sounded, at the time, like a form of goodbye; the sequel, in O'Leary's words again, was simply 'having fun with the horrific idea that David Bowie Is Old'. If anything, 'The Stars (Are Out Tonight)' was the comeback. He was full of life, wit and vigour; there was no hint that he only had a few years left.

So, while it may have seemed obvious with hindsight, there was no reason for critics to assume that 'Blackstar' and 'Lazarus' were a two-part farewell. References to ageing and death were threaded through his earlier work, and the videos showed him playing a character in settings shaped by science fiction, fantasy and horror. We don't see the rise and fall narrative of Ziggy Stardust as a biographical representation of David Bowie's life; so why should anyone have guessed that Button Eyes provided a window into David Jones's illness?

Even the definitive statement that *Blackstar* was a 'parting gift' was complicated by Visconti's further suggestion that Bowie was still working at the time of his death: he 'wrote and demo-ed five fresh songs, and was anxious to return to the studio one last time . . . and I thought, and *he* thought, that he'd have a few months, at least.' When he came up with the concept for the 'Lazarus' video, according to Renck, Bowie didn't know his cancer was terminal. 'I just want to make it a simple performance video,' he told Renck, who suggested that Bowie lie on a bed as a reference to the biblical figure Lazarus. They were still shooting when Bowie discovered that his treatment was to be stopped, and that the disease had won.

'I still don't know if he started making *Blackstar* before he knew he was ill, or after,' says Francis Whately, director of the 2017 documentary *The Last Five Years*.

People are so desperate for *Blackstar* to be this parting gift that Bowie made for the world when he knew he was dying but I think it's simplistic to think that. There is more ambiguity there than people want to acknowledge. I don't think he knew he was going to die.

However, he must have known there was a chance he wasn't going to recover, so to do an album with a certain amount of ambiguity in it, is Bowie playing the cat and mouse game that he always played.

So, are 'Lazarus' and 'Blackstar' (and *Lazarus* and *Blackstar*) Bowie's deliberate farewells? Nes. Yo. Inevitably, their themes and execution were influenced by his illness; but the evidence also strongly suggests that they were not meant to be his last releases. According to *Lazarus* co-author Enda Walsh, 'he had many, many more ideas of songs to write and books that he wanted to do. David was always going, ideas, ideas, ideas.' He was even, director Ivo van Hove says, planning a sequel to *Lazarus* after watching its debut. 'He wanted to continue and continue.' And of course, he did, even after death.

This chapter is just another interpretation and speculation, from the available evidence – we can't know what Bowie intended, and his intention is, in any case, never the full picture – but the reading it offers is more complex than the media narrative that dominated reviews after January 2016. It suggests that the final work of Bowie's life is not just about dying, but also about changing and continuing in a different form. As the name Lazarus suggests, it is about regeneration and new life, another theme that can be traced back through Bowie's work. Ziggy was officially killed off in June 1973, but stubbornly returned: Bowie performed under that name in October of the same year, for the *1980 Floor Show*. Aladdin Sane is his American reincarnation (or relocation – Ziggy hadn't really died, he'd just moved to the United States) and his distinctive visual image, with the crimson mullet haircut, persists until the cover of *Diamond Dogs*.

Major Tom, thought to be lost in space at the end of the 1960s, was brought back in 'Ashes to Ashes', in Neil Tennant's remix of 'Hallo Spaceboy', and arguably, as we'll see, also in the video for 'Blackstar'. The Bowie of Berlin is revisited in passing through Nathan Adler's diaries for *1. Outside* and again, more directly, in 'Where Are We Now?'. The Pierrot from 'Ashes to Ashes' reappears as a puppet in the 2013 video for 'Love Is Lost', alongside the Thin White Duke, who by nature never leaves for long: the first line of 'Station to Station' always announces his return. In a 2003 advertisement for Vittel, all his previous personae share a house with the older Bowie, drinking his mineral water, hogging the bathroom and blocking the stairs. 'And I'm running down the street of life!' he declares on the soundtrack. 'And I'm never gonna let you die!'

If Bowie was fascinated by death, he was also unwilling to destroy any of his old creations for ever; he kept them in that imaginary museum, the storehouse or warehouse of masks and costumes, and they were always there for him to retrieve. He was driven, in his earlier career, to move on, to ditch styles and genres, to constantly change and find a new hook, but he became a habitual plunderer of his own archive. Postmodern recycling may suggest a superficial appropriation of older culture, but it also revives, bringing new life to dead, lost and forgotten things. A person, and a practice, can contain opposites. Bowie embraced this kind of contradiction. He could play with two ideas at once, and switch between them at speed.

He could shift gears with a wink, within a lyrical line-break. 'Who said time is on my side?' he mournfully asked in 'Survive', from the 1999 *'hours...'* album. 'I've got ears and eyes, and nothing in my life.' But then, as Simon Critchley notes, the mood immediately changes to one of bold, bright affirmation. 'I'll survive your naked eyes,' he goes on, adding the firm repetition, 'I'll survive.' Critchley finds another uplifting message in 'I Can't Give Everything Away' from *Blackstar*, which was released posthumously as the third and final single from the album, in April 2016. 'Saying no but meaning yes . . . this is all I ever meant.' 'Within Bowie's negativity,' Critchley concludes, 'beneath his apparent naysaying and gloom, one can hear a clear *Yes*, an absolute and unconditional affirmation of life.'

Bowie's final portrait, taken by Jimmy King in autumn 2015 and released on his sixty-ninth birthday, testifies to this impulse. He stands against a New York street shutter in a sharp grey suit and hat, grinning broadly like a gangster who's just pulled off the biggest heist of his life; in another shot from the same sequence, he leaps forward at the camera, his mouth open in a laughing roar. As Joyce also wrote, at the end of *Ulysses*, 'yes I said yes I will Yes.' Accepting his age and the limits of his lifespan – no, he won't be around for ever in this mortal form – Bowie also offers an almighty yes, launching himself into what was left of his life, and into the afterlife beyond it.

There was, as we'll see, more to his 'parting gift' than the message that he was leaving. This was not just the resigned farewell note from a dying man. It was also the work of an artist who was seriously ill, desperately wanted to stay alive, and was preparing for the best and worst alternatives. On one level, it was a look back at his entire career, a survey of the inventory in his imaginary museum. *Blackstar* retrieves and repurposes diverse odds and ends, adapting aspects of his work from the last fifty years, from his first ever single to his most recent releases. It is an act of taking stock and, to an extent, a closing of the books. It says hello again to many of his previous selves: it calls them back and then fondly dismisses them; for now, and perhaps for ever. In the time he had left, he was able to consider and curate his legacy.

Throughout the decades, Bowie had experimented with the liminal zones between male and female, east and west, gay and straight, black and white. Through the multiple characters of 'Blackstar' and 'Lazarus', he explores the boundary between life and death, revisiting the past and facing his possible future. It included a message to his fans, but it went beyond a simple goodbye. Isn't that what we'd expect of him? Or as he says himself in 'Lazarus': 'Ain't that just like me?'

★

How did we get here? We can piece together a route through the mosaic of his life, from the global fame of the 1980s to his final months, in late 2015. Any summary of those decades is inevitably a simplification – every life is more complex than this – but we can plot a narrative and construct a story, with Bowie as the central character.

It was, he later claimed, the fear of death that had fuelled his manic energy throughout the 1960s and 1970s. 'Even as a young man, I was always aware that death was the one absolute certainty about life. It didn't reduce my feeling of buoyancy, it pushed me into a kind of colossal, obsessive activity.' We saw how it drove him – coupled, perhaps, with the constant fear of family schizophrenia at his back. He felt he had to keep moving, keep creating, keep up the momentum. That energy changed in the 1980s, as he became more cautious and pragmatic. Around the age of thirty-five, perhaps realising he was going to survive into his forties and beyond, he started to think more deliberately about his commercial future, and to work out how he could parlay his previous success into international mega-stardom. Rather than staying constantly ahead of the cultural moment, he tried to second-guess what the mainstream audience wanted, and increasingly – with *Tonight* (1984) and *Never Let Me Down* (1987) – his attempts fell flat. 'I was trying to be predictable,' he said with hindsight. 'But nobody wanted predictable.'

Between 1982 and 1992 his primary residence was the

Château du Signal, at the top of a forested hill in Lausanne, Switzerland. I walked up that hill, glimpsing his mansion through the trees, and along the banks of nearby Lake Geneva. It's very beautiful, very peaceful, very expensive and very isolated. He saved on tax, but became cut off and stagnated. By his own admission, using a characteristic metaphor of himself as a sailor: 'I lost the trade winds and found myself in the creative doldrums. I was pandering to a certain audience.' His collaborators at the time reported that he was bored out of his skull and climbing the walls.

And then David Bowie found happiness, and let it shine through into his next LP. *Black Tie White Noise*, from 1993, is essentially a wedding album, commemorating his relationship with Iman; they were married in April of the previous year. 'Morning star, you're beautiful,' he sings unselfconsciously on 'Miracle Goodnight'. It's the sound of contentment. Fortunately, Iman found Château du Signal too quiet, preferring city life, and the new couple put their mansion on the market.

Black Tie White Noise was followed by a return to his Bromley roots, to enjoy the freedom of an esoteric side project: the soundtrack for a BBC adaptation of Hanif Kureishi's *The Buddha of Suburbia*. Kureishi had set up a meeting to ask simply if they could use some of Bowie's old songs. Bowie said he'd write new music instead. The pressure was off, and he began to experiment again. 'I've got to start making records for myself rather than other people,' he told Dylan Jones in 1994.

1. Outside, released in 1995, was the edited version of a sprawling futuristic epic, with Bowie playing multiple characters from a female villain to a child victim, from an old man to a Minotaur. It was genuinely about playing, this time, rather than becoming: Ramona A. Stone and Nathan Adler didn't consume him the way Ziggy had. He was having fun. His next public persona was a ragged magician in Alexander McQueen outfits, his eyes ringed with black and hair a bright copper. This character was never named, but a line in 'The Hearts Filthy Lesson' – 'who's been wearing Miranda's clothes?' – always led me to think of him as Prospero, from Shakespeare's *The Tempest*, working his last magic before breaking his staff.

This impish energy lasted through the drum 'n' bass of Bowie's fiftieth birthday year, through *Earthling* and its album tour, and then was formally killed off in 1999 on the cover of '*hours...*' where the Prospero figure lies in the arms of an angelic, longer-haired David, staring up at his successor. A ceremonial handing-over at the turn of the millennium. Finally, with the pantomime out of his system, Bowie was ready to play the role of mature curator. And then in August of the new century, his daughter Alexandria Zahra Jones was born, and everything changed again.

Bowie had still been hoovering up 'huge amounts of coke'

in the early 1990s, according to psychologist Oliver James (quoted in Dylan Jones's compendium of interviews). 'This was just before Iman, of course.' He was still chain-smoking through the nineties, too, though he'd scaled down from his 1970s brand, Gitanes, to Marlboro Lights: he was on forty a day in 1997, he confessed to Jarvis Cocker in a *Big Issue* interview. 'I should go even lighter, I suppose, because I know I'm going to have to give up sooner or later when the kid comes.' It was the last of his vices. 'I smoke like a chimney,' he admitted at the end of the decade. 'But that's about it. I do Tylenol, but nothing else. I don't do *anything* any more, I don't drink, I don't do drugs.'

He finally quit completely: by the end of 1999, or by December 2001, depending on who you listen to and who you believe. He now woke up at 5 a.m. each day, before the baby; he meditated regularly, and worked out with a boxing trainer. His personal chef kept him on a healthy diet. He took cholesterol pills on his doctor's orders. A new regime for a new millennium. Typically, he even rewrote his own history, telling Kate Moss that he'd 'not really' taken drugs when he was younger. He wanted to purify his past self, too.

He wanted to live: to live long, and live well, for Lexi's sake. They'd already had a scare on 11 September, when Bowie called Iman just as the second plane hit the World Trade Center: she was in Manhattan with the baby, while he was recording upstate. 'Get the pram,' he ordered her down the phone. 'Get the hell out of there.' She took the pram and ran twenty blocks with it. Later, David visited Ground Zero and wrote a song describing the 'great white scar over Battery Park'. It became 'New Killer Star', which opened 2003's *Reality* album. The accompanying tour was his last.

Despite the new health regime, his body was starting to betray him. First it was a simple sore throat, leading him to miss easy notes on 'China Girl'. He threw down the mike stand in disgust. He wasn't used to this. 'What, you don't think the last twenty-five, thirty years has taken a toll?' asked Mike Garson, his long-term pianist. The throat troubles were followed by a bout of flu, causing him to cancel dates in December 2003. During a set in Oslo he was hit in the eye with a lollipop thrown from the crowd: 'You bastard. Do remember I've only got one. The other one's just become a little more decorative than it was before.' Then in Prague he struggled through 'Reality', left the stage in obvious pain, and came back to apologise, blaming a trapped nerve in his shoulder. He finished the set sitting on a stool. After his next gig, in Germany, he was taken straight to hospital for an angioplasty, with stents placed in his arteries. His bandmates agree he'd suffered a heart attack on stage, though it was never officially confirmed.

Other sources suggest that this was neither the first time nor the last. Guitarist Reeves Gabrels knew Bowie had dealt with chest pains for years, but 'he swore me to secrecy . . .

I should have told Iman.' Wendy Leigh claims that Bowie suffered six heart attacks in the years leading up to his death; she got the information from 'someone very close to him'. Bowie clearly dealt with serious illness by covering it up and keeping it to himself. He'd become adept at separating his personal life from the public image, and controlling his media narrative. If he could maintain the lie that his health was fine, then maybe, on one level, it would become the truth.

By now, he was a New Yorker by default. It wasn't planned: it took him by surprise. 'I've lived in New York longer than I've lived anywhere else,' he realised in 2003. 'It's amazing.' He got to know Nolita and SoHo, his new territory. He knew when to go out; he knew when to stay in. He'd wave across the street at Moby, chat to other dads in the local park, grab a grilled chicken sandwich with watercress from Olive's on Prince Street, pick up a bag of oranges on the way home. The ten years of his unofficial retirement, between the *Reality* tour and *The Next Day*, were very different from his earlier decades: it was a good life, but the pace was transformed. The old energy had shifted. He wasn't in a rush any more. 'Having a family levelled me out,' he explained. 'I'll tell you what a lot of it is; it's moving from a life of action to one of a little more contemplation. Initially, every minute of your life has to count, and you have to be doing something.' Now, aware of his own physical vulnerability, he just wanted to make it last.

'I just wanna be there for Alexandria,' he told a newspaper in 2003. 'I desperately want to live forever. You know what I want . . . to still be around in another forty or fifty years. She's so exciting and lovely so I want to be around when she grows up.' He was doing everything he could to stay alive, even while his body conspired against him. He scaled down, took things much more quietly. 'He was keeping himself to himself,' explained photographer Mick Rock, his friend since 1972. 'At the time everyone thought he was dying, but he was just not doing anything.'

I spent a couple of weeks in New York during December 2015, just before he died, visiting his favourite shops, cafés and bars. Washington Square Park, the Vesuvio Bakery on Prince Street, Dean & DeLuca's delicatessen, McNally Jackson booksellers, the Café Gitane and Caffe Reggio. He used to slum it here, wearing a hoodie and flat cap, carrying a Greek newspaper as a disguise. It was December, and I was following the strict schedule of my research year, so I was still wearing my custom-made duplicate of the McQueen jacket from *Earthling*, with a goatee beard and black eyeliner. Unlike Bowie, who dressed down to disappear, I was in full costume, a tribute act: an unconscious echo of him dressing up as Warhol and enjoying the double-takes from Manhattanites, twenty years before. Someone stopped me on the street to compliment me on my outfit. 'Looking out of a window and watching people is quite enough to keep me occupied for half an hour,' Bowie once said of his life in New York. If he'd glanced down from his window at that moment, from his apartment high on 285 Lafayette, he would have seen me.

It was a good life. I enjoyed my taste of it. Bookshops, coffee, independent record stores and gigs: he never tired of discovering new music, and sneaked anonymously, alone, into concerts, standing at the back. One evening towards the end of my stay, I had cocktails in the Crosby Bar, then dinner at Indochine – knowing Bowie had taken Iman to both – before walking to the New York Theatre Workshop for a performance of *Lazarus*. I took my seat in the second row, just before the lights went down. Sophia Anne Caruso, who played the Girl, later tweeted that she'd seen me and thought I was a Bowie revenant, a return of his late nineties incarnation. It was generous of her.

By that point, of course, everything had already changed. I just didn't know it. Most people didn't know it. 'He had told very, very few people about his illness,' recalled Johan Renck. 'Even people in his closest sphere didn't know. He told because he had to.' With hindsight he looks frail and old in the photographs from the opening night of *Lazarus*, a few weeks earlier on 7 December, but then, everything about Bowie's final months seems obvious with hindsight. Candy Clark, who played Mary-Lou in *The Man Who Fell to Earth*, missed the musical but saw the pictures. 'He looked like he was in pain, and kinda yellow. Jaundiced. Dry. That should have been a clue.' There were so many clues, only visible after his death.

Enda Walsh knew about the cancer, but even he had to guess about Bowie's internal battles. 'Can you imagine the last moments of your life . . . to have that grief and fight with yourself, wanting to live, wanting to continue, but wanting rest . . . how do you deal with the fact you're not going to be here in three months?'

Suddenly, in secret, after all those years of taking it carefully and easily, Bowie's relationship with time had shifted again. There was a deadline now. The pace had changed. The pressure was back on. He had so many possible projects he'd never finished: a *Ziggy Stardust* musical, a sequel to *Lazarus*, the extra tracks that didn't make it onto the album, perhaps the semi-fictional autobiography he'd half started in the 1970s. Chris O'Leary imagines his thought process: 'frantically writing, settling the accounts, trying to keep the balls in the air. New titles, names, chord changes. Another play – maybe *1984* at last! *2. Outside: Infection!* Should write Brian. More albums . . . More, always more.'

O'Leary's monologue is invented; like any theory of Bowie's intentions and motivations, including my own, it's a mixture of speculation and fact, based on the available evidence. But as O'Leary knows, Bowie did write to Brian Eno. 'It ended with this sentence: "Thank you for our good times . . . they will never rot." And it was signed "Dawn". I realise now he was saying goodbye.' If the co-creator of *Low* only realised after the fact, we can't blame ourselves for missing the hidden messages in Bowie's last release.

My research year had started off as a personal experiment and become a media story. It was always slightly ridiculous; after Bowie's death, it risked seeming tasteless. It was even more important to me, at that point, that I retained its structure and discipline. I needed to keep to the rules, or it would fall apart, and my project would end. In January 2016 I was still symbolically inhabiting Bowie's early 2000s period. I'd allowed myself to see *Lazarus* in New York as a one-off experience, even though it disrupted the time-scheme, but listening to *Blackstar* would break my self-imposed continuity. So I bought the album, and shelved it. I didn't listen to it until five months after Bowie's death. Then I played the whole LP, on headphones, once; afterwards, I put it away again for two years. I found it too personal, too painful, to listen to as if it were a normal record. I only took it off the shelf again to write this chapter.

Blackstar presents us with new Bowie territory; a new map, a new matrix that expands and builds upon our previous knowledge of him. As online discussions demonstrate, its leads can be followed in multiple directions. We saw how a relatively short, simple song like 'The Man Who Sold the World' works as an encyclopaedia of links, its references taking us out across multiple levels of meaning; where can we even start with an entire album, and where do we finish?

Let's start with the black star itself. While, as some fans pointed out, the ★ symbol is decipherable as the Unicode character 'U+2605', a possible reference to Mick Ronson's birthday, we can reasonably assert that it represents Bowie himself: the star replaces him on the cover – the first time he hasn't been pictured on a studio album – and his name, below it, is spelled out through its parts. Placed together, the stylised B, O, W, I and E would overlap and reform into the complete symbol. It also recalls the blue and red lightning bolt that came to signify Bowie after *Aladdin Sane* – a final full stop underneath that energetic exclamation mark – and, of course, serves as a dark shadow to Ziggy Stardust and all the other stellar references in Bowie's work: 'The Prettiest Star', 'New Killer Star', 'The Stars (Are Out Tonight)'. Other possible echoes – 'black star' as the medical term for a breast cancer lesion, the 1960 Elvis Presley song 'Black Star', warning of death – reinforce those associations.

The album art includes, above the lyrics of 'Girl Loves Me', a reproduction of the 'Pioneer plaque', a pictorial message included on two spacecraft, intended to explain their origins if they were intercepted by extraterrestrial life. They were launched in 1972, the year of Ziggy's arrival. The plaque features a schematic representation of a hydrogen reaction, simplified images of a man and woman, a diagram of the solar system, and a map of radiating lines, showing the relation of the sun to a series of pulsars (also called a white dwarf – a dense, dying star). Bowie and designer Jonathan Barnbrook draw on the Pioneer plaque's visual style throughout the album booklet: suns, novas and comic-book flashes explode on the pages, and the lyrics of 'Blackstar' itself are displayed like constellations, linked by thin lines into astrological patterns.

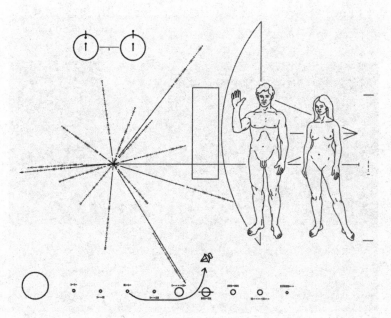

The Pioneer plaque is a guide to interpretation. Its symbols represent real-world referents in simplified form: a circle with a horizontal line through it, for instance, stands for the actual planet Saturn, in all its three-dimensional complexity. On this basis, what kind of astronomical phenomenon does the black-star symbol signify? Surely it can only be the eclipse that appears in the fifth shot of the 'Blackstar' video, just as the drum kicks in and Bowie's vocal begins. We've been offered four fragmented close-ups of the stranded astronaut, and now see his location in a long shot: he is lying back against the jagged rocks of a bleak planet, under an obscured sun. A ring of light escapes behind a dark disc. Here is the blackstar, 'at the centre of it all': the heart of the album.

'At the centre of it all,' the lyric continues, 'your eyes.' And with the verse 'How many times does an angel fall', we watch a fifteen-second sequence showing Bowie's eyes in close-up, then those of a woman, in an exchange of glances.

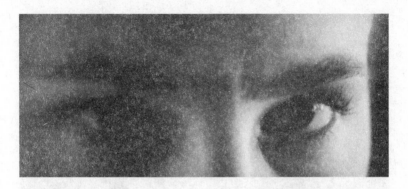

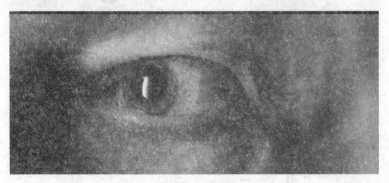

His left pupil, of course, is enlarged, a visual match with the black disc of the eclipse. The distinctive eye is, in turn, a visual shorthand for Bowie himself; as much part of his distinctive brand image as the *Aladdin Sane* lightning bolt. The linguistic echo between 'eye' and 'I' provides another punning confirmation, and the album artwork supports the idea by placing a symbol of an eye and a star on the lyric page for 'Lazarus'. Bowie is the blackstar symbol; the blackstar symbol is realised as the eclipse; the eclipse matches

Bowie's eye; Bowie's eye stands for Bowie himself. We have come full circle; and indeed, in a shot of the priest character, he rotates a book with a blackstar cover in front of himself, in a slow orbit, until the symbol covers his face.

The refrain 'I'm a blackstar' further confirms this link between Bowie and the eclipse, as it defines the term through a series of denials. He's a blackstar, but he's not a white star. He's not a film star, not a gang-star. Among all these nega-tives is a single positive: he's a star star. A blackstar, then, is defined within the song as a double star, two elements combined into one, like the book obscuring Bowie's face during its rotation. Again, the idea returns us to the eclipse, where one sphere is laid over another of almost identical size. It also fits perfectly with Bowie's history of doppelgangers and alter egos, and the split selves in his videos, including both 'Blackstar' and 'Lazarus', and further recalls the dupli-cated vocals of his songs – again, including 'Blackstar', where

Bowie's voice is artificially raised in pitch and double-tracked against itself in an eerie echo. The song's two musical themes work in the same overlapping dynamic: towards the end, the slower chant slowly emerges from the upbeat bragging ('I'm a blackstar, way up on money, I got game'), beginning almost inaudibly but rising until it dominates the final minutes.

Crucially, though, the effect of this duplication and doubling is not deletion but addition and creation: an eclipse can only exist through overlap. We can still see the light behind the dark; in fact, we can only see the black disc because of the halo escaping it. Rather than cancelling each other out, they coexist through contrast, defining each other by what they're not, like the twinned vocals, the interlocking musical sections and the split personae. Bowie's vocal is the 'low voice' of the track only in relation to its higher-pitched duplicate. Button Eyes is distinguished from the priest only by their props: bandages and a book respectively.

This image at the core of 'Blackstar' is fundamental to the album's meaning, but to understand its implications fully we have to look back to the cover of Bowie's previous release, *The Next Day*. In collaboration with the same designer, Jonathan Barnbrook, Bowie wanted to reuse but subvert his own history. They experimented with various possibilities, including a Mickey Mouse silhouette over the *Pin Ups* portrait, and scribbles over the iconic *Aladdin Sane* image, before settling on the cover of '*Heroes*', a blank white square covering most of Bowie's face, and the title crossed out with a plain black line.

In each of the examples, the point was to conceal and obscure, but to leave the original recognisable beneath the added graphic: much like an eclipse. If the white square of *The Next Day* was too big, hiding too much of the *'Heroes'* cover art, any sense of subversion would have been lost. Instead, the past and present are perfectly balanced. Bowie's 1977 album escapes from around the white square, visible but subtly altered, and the original title is legible beneath the neat line.

He'd used this technique before – long before, on the cover of 1980's *Scary Monsters*, and on his previous collaboration with Jonathan Barnbrook, for the *Heathen* album. *Scary Monsters* announces a break with the 'Berlin trilogy' by recycling the cover of *'Heroes'* alongside *Low* and *Lodger*, and partially defacing them with white paint: rough brushwork in this case, rather than a neat square. *Heathen* anticipates the design of *The Next Day* in a different way, through the text of its interior album art. Verses from the title track, written in a distinctive font, are neatly crossed through, but still readable: '~~& when the sun is low~~ / ~~And the rays high~~ / ~~I can see it now~~ / ~~I can feel it die~~.'

The technique evokes a theoretical strategy used by Jacques Derrida, whose work we encountered in Chapter Two. Nicholas Pegg claims that Derrida is one of Bowie's 'favoured philosophers', so its use may be entirely deliberate; but even if it's coincidental or unconscious, his adoption of this specific crossing-through technique, whether with white paint, a blank square or a black line, helps us to understand the dynamic between binaries, duplicates and oppositions – between past and present, absence and presence, living and dead – that structures *Blackstar*.

Derrida would say that the crossed-out term is held 'under erasure', still clearly visible despite the strikethrough, but subtly changed. We can recognise the cover of *'Heroes'* on *The Next Day* – that's the whole point – but equally importantly, we can see that it's not the 1977 original. The result is not absence or presence, but something in between. The origin, says Derrida, 'must make its necessity felt before letting itself be erased. It is in fact contradictory . . . the trace is not only the disappearance of origin . . . it means that the origin did not even disappear.'

A 'trace' is an alternative meaning, held in a limbo of absent presence. To Derrida, this awareness of what something is *not* structures all language: 'cat' has a specific meaning because it is not 'bat', 'bot', 'cot', 'cab' and so on. 'Without a trace retaining the other as other in the same,' he writes, 'no difference would do its work and no meaning would appear.' The meaning of 'cat' depends on it not being those other possible sounds, which therefore remain part of its definition: we have selected it from a series of similar possibilities. We've already encountered this concept, in fact, through the main characters of 'Blackstar', who are dressed and styled identically, defined by a minor but significant difference like the 'a' in 'cat' and the 'o' in 'cot': Button Eyes is identifiable by his bandages and the priest figure carries a book. The third persona, described by Renck as the 'flamboyant trickster' (first seen when he delivers the line 'Something happened on the day he died'), is distinguished by his absence of either prop. Bowie's long list of what a blackstar *isn't* (a gang-star, a marvel star, a porn star, a wandering star) echoes this idea.

His puns and wordplay depend on the same dynamic. 'Space Oddity' only works as a joke because we are aware of *2001: A Space Odyssey*: the original title hovers there, in absent presence. We could convey this, following Derrida's example, by writing it as ~~A Space Odyssey~~. The first line of 'Blackstar' also carries a ghost alternative, a possible lyric that Bowie decided against: his earlier choice was 'In the villa of all men', not 'Ormen'. 'Dollar Days', from Blackstar, confesses, 'I'm trying to, I'm dying to', with a melancholy double meaning: 'I'm dying too.' Once we're aware of it, it is hard not to hear those words: they remain crossed out, but not fully erased.

The Next Day, as we saw, draws explicitly on this idea in its cover design: it is, literally, ~~'Heroes'~~, its typography matched by the obscured image. *Scary Monsters* does the same through its defaced cover art, depicting ~~Low,~~ ~~'Heroes'~~ and ~~Lodger~~: it announces itself as a departure from the previous albums, while also bringing them inevitably to mind. Even when Bowie opts not to mention his previous work, reviewers will do it for him; in the classic, clichéd example, every new LP was always compared to *Scary Monsters*. But critics can't be blamed for recalling his previous albums as a point of reference: the very idea of change and transformation, so central to his career, relies on a transition from one mode to another.

Our sense of *Young Americans* is partly shaped by its contrast with *Diamond Dogs*, as Bowie abandoned science-fiction glam and rebranded himself as a blue-eyed soul man. The 'Berlin

Bowie' of *Low* is, in turn, seen as a shift from the cocaine-fuelled, occult-obsessed Bowie of Los Angeles and *Station to Station*. *Blackstar's* experimental jazz is, as reviews noted, quite different from the rock of *The Next Day*: in this respect, just as *The Next Day* presented itself visually as ~~'Heroes'~~, *Blackstar* is ~~The Next Day~~. We are always subtly aware of his other albums as points of comparison and difference. They remain the 'trace' against which his other work is defined.

This dynamic runs through Bowie's relationship to his past; to the personae, costumes and masks of his previous work. As we saw, though he drops and discards them, and sometimes even attempts to kill them off, they remain in the storehouse, always retrievable and potentially available for recycling. They, too, are present in absence. Major Tom was presumed lost in 1969, then returned in 1980, and cameoed in the 1996 remix of 'Hallo Spaceboy': in between, we could write his name as ~~Major Tom~~, held in limbo. Bowie's old selves are neither alive nor dead, but under temporary erasure: obscured but still visible, like sunlight during an eclipse.

This concept of absent presence is central to the entire *Blackstar* album. If *The Next Day* – and specifically 'Where Are We Now?' – was a hail and farewell to the Berlin Bowie of *'Heroes'*, *Blackstar* says hello again and goodbye, for now and perhaps for ever, to a wider encyclopaedia of references from Bowie's previous career. He's re-entered his storehouse, his imaginary museum, to explore the artefacts from his younger days – no coincidence, surely, that he'd recently helped the V&A to prepare their exhibition of his life and work – and emerges with an armful of trophies, which he adapts for this album in a slightly different but still recognisable form. Like *The Next Day*, this is a revisiting that also carries the melancholy possibility of a final goodbye. Bowie knew, putting *Blackstar* together, that this might be the last time he recovered those old memories and played with his old props.

So the future slang of 'Girl Loves Me', tweaked from Anthony Burgess's fictional language Nadsat, says hello again, and goodbye for now, to the novel and film of *A Clockwork Orange*, which inspired the interior cover art of *Ziggy Stardust* and gave Bowie the line 'droogie, don't crash here,' from 'Suffragette City'. In the 'Girl Loves Me' lyric, it's mixed with Polari, the gay slang popular in the 1960s and 1970s. Hi again – *bona to vada* – and goodbye to that, too, for now and perhaps for ever.

Hello again to 'Fashion', as the dancers in 'Blackstar' incorporate one of Bowie's moves from its 1980 video into their juddering choreography. Hello and goodbye to the New York of 9/11, alluded to as 'the centre of it all' in 2002's 'Slow Burn': the phrase is, of course, central again to 'Blackstar'. Hello and goodbye to another memory from the Berlin period, 'A New Career in a New Town': 'I Can't Give Everything Away' reprises the *Low* track with its mournful harmonica.

Welcome back, *Station to Station*: the striped blue and white suit from the album cover is recovered from history's wardrobe for Bowie to wear again in the 'Lazarus' video. 'What about if we reawaken this guy?' he asked the director, Johan Renck. The Thin White Duke returned again.

There was 'no deliberate, underlying, firm quest to have any references to past times', Renck claimed in one interview, while in another he admitted to telling Bowie, 'It's almost impossible to make a video with you without mirroring elements of your various iterations over the years . . . it was all his own myth.' Perhaps it wasn't deliberate, then, but unavoidable. If you tug on a thread, the costume follows. When we retrieve *Station to Station* from the archive, the occult associations tumble out with it: Renck is a self-confessed 'huge Crowley fan', and the videos for 'Lazarus' and 'Blackstar', as we'll see, both involve elements of magical ritual.

Hello again to Bowie's 1960s girlfriend Hermione Farthingale, through a playful chain of references: the 'Where Are We Now' video referenced her movie role in *Song of Norway*, and 'Blackstar', with its opening evocation of the village called Ørmen, is itself a 'song of Norway'. Farewell to German Expressionism, which Bowie studied in the mid-1970s, and which inspired the stark lighting of his Thin White Duke tours; the figure in the striped suit was named 'somnambulist' in his sketch notes, leading us back to the murderous sleepwalker Cesare in Robert Wiene's 1920 film

The Cabinet of Dr Caligari. And there's a sense of closure in the call-back to *Nineteen Eighty-Four* on 'Girl Loves Me', with the line 'I'm sitting in the chestnut tree': the Chestnut Tree Café is where we leave Winston Smith at the end of the novel.

Goodbye to Elvis, too – born on the same day as Bowie, twelve years apart – through the tribute to his 1960 single 'Black Star'. We can follow this reference back to *The Buddha of Suburbia*, where Bowie hubristically crowned himself as a home-grown version of the King – 'Elvis is English and climbs the hills' – and then move forward again to 'Dollar Days', where he again imagines the country he left behind as a kind of Jerusalem. 'If I'll never see the English evergreens I'm running to . . . it's nothing to me. It's nothing to see.' We might also look sideways at the title 'Dollar Days' and see it as a punning take on 'Golden Years', the track Bowie supposedly wrote for Elvis. Presley, or so the story goes, was so impressed he telephoned immediately, asking the younger singer to produce his next record. The collaboration never happened: Presley died six months after the phone call.

There are nods to Bowie's friends and collaborators Damien Hirst and Alexander McQueen in the jewelled skull of 'Blackstar'. There's an unmistakable visual echo of Jim Henson's *Labyrinth*, in which Bowie played Jareth the Goblin King, in the fantasy landscapes of 'Blackstar', and there's a hint of cocaine snorting, the soundtrack to his 1970s, in the opening seconds before ''Tis a Pity She Was a Whore'. Goodbye to all that.

Hello again to a song from his recent history: 'Sue (Or in a Season of Crime)', his single from the 2014 *Nothing Has Changed* compilation album, which was re-recorded for *Blackstar*. Its breakbeats now recall 'Little Wonder' and 'Battle for Britain', from the drum 'n' bass period of 1997. Critics mocked him for it at the time, but now they're praising his experimental vibe. So it goes. And hello to a song from the distant past: 'Sue / I never dreamed', runs the lyric. 'I Never Dreamed' was the first track Bowie ever recorded, with The Konrads, in 1963.

'Sue . . . goodbye', the song concludes. Hello and goodbye. He's retrieved so much from the storehouse on this occasion; he's arranged it into new patterns, shaped it to fit his current direction with Donny McCaslin and his jazz group. (Hello again to jazz, too: the saxophone had been Bowie's first instrument, and it was his half-brother Terry who introduced him to the genre, back in Plaistow Grove.) Those styles, masks and voices are integrated into the mosaic of *Blackstar*, some of them so well concealed they almost disappear: they're embedded for fans to find, for people with too much time on their hands. 'He had enormous loyalty to his fans,' Renck confirms. 'He would do things to please his fans, or to tease his fans: "They're going to question this. They won't know what this is about. They're going to have a lot of fun thinking about this."'

If *Black Tie White Noise* was a wedding album, this is a

souvenir album, with the past scattered throughout. 'I Can't Give Everything Away', the final track, holds a double meaning, too. It's a kind of apology – he can't reveal all his secrets – but equally, it's an admission that he can't let the past go. He brings his history back, then half hides it, present in absence. 'Saying no but meaning yes, this is all I ever meant. That's the message that I sent.' The man on the Pioneer plaque raises his right hand in an ambiguous greeting, and the album art also features a constellation that can be joined up into the figure of a star man, his left hand aloft. *Aloha*, as Elvis might have put it. Hello and goodbye. Or as Bowie phrased it himself in 2002, on his farewell tribute to his late father, 'Everyone Says Hi'. The raised palm embraces and allows for both possibilities.

Hello again and goodbye, finally, to Major Tom. Johan Renck both confirmed and denied any deliberate reference to the hero of 'Space Oddity'. 'To me, it was one hundred percent Major Tom,' he stated confidently in one interview, while evading the question in another: 'Most things like this are for the eyes of the beholder, you know? You make of it whatever you want.' Bowie, inevitably, declined to comment; but the astronaut is surely confirmed as Major Tom through another series of intertextual references. His smiley-face badge links him to the artificial intelligence, GERTY, who oversees the lunar base in Duncan Jones's *Moon* (2009): GERTY communicates through a calm solicitous voice (provided by Kevin

Spacey) and a limited set of emoticons, displaying a beaming, crying or puzzled yellow face to roughly match his mood.

GERTY, in turn, is clearly indebted to *2001's* HAL, from their measured vocal tones and simple visual cues (a red, unblinking eye in HAL's case) to their patronising approach to the human astronauts. *2001: A Space Odyssey*, of course, was the original inspiration for 'Space Oddity'. The connections are too perfect to resist: Bowie was both paying tribute to his son and acknowledging their shared influence by revisiting the hero of his first hit song. Again, though, there's an ambiguity in this act of retrieval, as Tom is already dead at the start of 'Blackstar': brought back and killed off in the same moment. As a jewelled skull in a spacesuit, the Major is present but absent under the eclipse.

So *Blackstar* is, in part, a cataloguing of where Bowie's been: a coded best-of compilation, built around this yes/no, hi/bye dynamic of calling back the past to celebrate it, change it, and, in Tom's case, let it drift into the void. In announcing its radical difference from his previous work, *Blackstar* inevitably defines itself against that oeuvre, and in departing from his past, it also takes stock of history.

It revisits some of his old themes, too, exploring the spaces between binaries of gender, race and age. 'Blackstar' has Bowie, now a white-haired, wrinkled white man, telling us, in African-American vernacular, 'I got game', and 'take your sedatives, boo.' He'd been inspired by Kendrick Lamar's hybrid hip-hop album *To Pimp a Butterfly*, released earlier in 2015, though there's also another possible throwaway pun in that 'boo': a playful scare. 'Blackstar' also features a woman with a tail, which Bowie told Renck, was 'kind of sexual'. It was a 'comment about gender', Jonathan Barnbrook suggests. 'Strange non-female or non-male-specific characters.' They'd been talking a lot, he remembers, about 'the way gender is moving around these days'. 'Man, she punched me like a dude', Bowie muses on ''Tis a Pity She Was a Whore'.

'Girl Loves Me' builds another gender hybrid into the line 'devotchka watch her garbles': he's modified the Nadsat word to make it scan better, but 'devotchka' is a girl, and 'yarbles', in *A Clockwork Orange*, are testicles. Bowie was playing with those oppositions – the devotchka could be another 'mama-papa', whose own mother's 'not sure if you're a boy or a girl' – right up to the end.

He'd confronted the contrast between his own youth and increasing age before, in 'Thursday's Child', 'The Stars (Are Out Tonight)' and the Vittel commercial; and he'd explored the life/death binary too – implicitly, when Ziggy refused to stay down, and explicitly, in the video to 'Bring Me the Disco King', where he digs up his own body – but never with this sense of immediacy. In 'Lazarus', Button Eyes returns, now writhing on what we assume to be his deathbed, while a new character, the somnambulist of his sketches, emerges from the wardrobe wearing the striped *Station to Station* outfit, and sashays, then scribbles, with theatrically frantic impatience. This slick, svelte figure, evoking the camp Bowie of the 1970s, literally comes back out of the closet, declaring, 'I was looking for your ass!' Bowie recognised the irony, and, according to Renck, 'started giggling like mad' at the idea. 'Fuck yeah, we've got to do that. Let's do that right away.'

Rather than two separate characters, they represent a split personality – the dying man (who we could read as 'Jones'), imprisoned in a weak body and flinging his arms about in frustration, and his active alter ego (by implication, 'Bowie'), still buzzing with ideas that need to be recorded while there's still time. Perhaps he's jotting down new plans; perhaps he's taking stock, writing a record of what's gone before. This is the side of Bowie who 'wanted to continue and continue'; or, in Enda Walsh's words, was 'wanting to continue, but wanting rest . . . how do you deal with the fact you're not going to be here in three months?'

Bowie dealt with it the way he'd always dealt with his inner demons: by throwing them outward into his art, in the spirit of German Expressionism. Button Eyes and the somnambulist are stylised, almost parodic figures: larger than life personae like Ziggy Stardust and the Thin White Duke, rather than straightforward self-portraits. The bedridden man is a shock-headed invalid, like an image of old age from a Victorian moral fable, and the sleepwalker is the embodiment of a queen bitch. Both of them, despite their differences, are driven by the same desperate urgency.

A skull, perhaps Major Tom's, sits on the somnambulist's desk – a memento mori, reminding him that his creative scribbling has a literal deadline – while a hand reaches out from under Button Eyes's bed, threatening to pull him under. The writer keeps glancing over at the bed, checking on the patient. He knows their fates are linked. 'Ain't that just like me?' Button Eyes cries, and he's right; the other man is just like him: they are two aspects of the same individual. Fittingly, they share the song's bridge with no shift in their vocals: the somnambulist sassily delivers the line 'By the time I got to New York', and Button Eyes shouts, 'then I used up all my money'.

But their differences are as important as their similarity. Button Eyes is confined, struggling to rise from his bed, while the sleepwalker can dance with fluid ease and write at accelerated speed. When Button Eyes collapses, shaking, and the fingers flex again beneath his bed, the somnambulist returns to his work with renewed intensity, reaching the bottom of the page and starting again. Finally, he takes a frustrated look back at the other man, accepts that his time outside the closet is over, and retreats backwards into it, closing the door. But we never see the wardrobe fully shut, at either the beginning or the end. The vulnerable body of David Jones may be entering its final stages, but his vibrantly theatrical alter ego, retaining all the vitality of his most creative decade, has simply stepped back into the shadows, leaving the possibilities open.

Bowie is exploring both sides of the binary here, facing the prospect of his own mortality and considering the legacy that will continue after he's gone. Button Eyes prepares for death even while he's still alive – 'Look up here, I'm in heaven,' he declares, as the camera stares down at him in his bed – but the other figure, the somnambulist, is proof that Bowie's former personae can be brought back from storage as easily as retrieving a costume from a wardrobe or a warehouse, an exhibition or museum. Like all Bowie's recycled references to his own earlier work, the sleepwalker is not exactly the same as his earlier incarnation on the cover of *Station to Station* – he's changed over time, and adapted for this new role, forty years later – but his spirit is undiminished. 'Jones' is on his last legs, but 'Bowie' will carry on.

This dynamic also underlies the video for 'Blackstar', but with an additional dimension. Here, the cast is increased, including younger acolytes alongside the multiple Bowie personae. The wanderer with a tail who discovers Tom's skull takes it back to her community, where, as the lyric specifies, 'only women kneel and smile'; and all three Bowie characters – Button Eyes, the priest and the trickster – interact with the same three dancers, several decades his junior. The two men are shirtless; one is pale and blond, and one dark-skinned. The third is a woman with brunette bobbed hair, wearing a white shirt beneath a blue dress.

They watch him preach, gazing reverently as he raises the tattered book with the black star on the cover – perhaps his life's work compiled in a single volume – then mouth the words 'I'm a blackstar.' Visconti remembers that he and Bowie discussed how they could change his voice for this line, to 'make one person sound like many people, in many different contexts, and many different spatial areas'. It's still Bowie's vocal, but he's spread himself further, dispersing his identity into a chorus. He cries out 'loud into the crowd', and they respond en masse. In a later shot, to reinforce the point, a new female disciple leans directly into the foreground and repeats the line with a hand at her mouth as amplifier. The priest taught the lesson, and others have taken up the call.

A ritual builds momentum in the 'Blackstar' video, as Tom's skull is placed on the back of one of the female villagers, who perform an urgent, jerky dance. In a nearby field, three scarecrows – one of them Bowie in a fourth guise? – writhe and grimace, and a monstrous creature approaches through the crops. Renck describes it as 'death . . . this sort of wraith that is summoned'. The three scarecrows resemble Christ and the two thieves crucified next to him, although 'at the centre of it all' is borrowed almost directly from Crowley: 'Let him then return to the Centre, and so to the Centre of all.' The ceremony's sources are both Christian and occult, then, with aspects of folklore and science-fiction fantasy. It may be a form of funeral for the lost astronaut, or a warding spell to protect the village from the monster in the fields, or, as Renck suggests, a summoning. Its details are, like the rest of the scenario, left deliberately obscure: the important point is ritual as an underlying theme.

Both videos face up to the prospect of impending death, whether it manifests as a wraith or a pale hand beneath the bed, and both explore a different, magical strategy for dealing with it. 'Lazarus', by splitting Bowie into two stylised figures

– a weakened and diminished old man, and a restless sleep-walker – suggests that the creative energy of his younger years can be called back from its closet, and that this side of him will continue when his physical body gives up the ghost: the door is left open, and the past can always be retrieved from the warehouse. 'Blackstar' takes a different approach, with its repeated motifs of spreading the word and handing on a message to younger followers. His legacy, it's implied, is placed in their hands; they voice his words and repeat his example. And of course, the message is also conveyed through glances; at the centre of it all are his eyes.

Exactly halfway through the video, at precisely five minutes into its ten-minute length, Bowie's eyes are intercut with those of a woman, perhaps one of the acolytes. It's a process of exchange: exchanged glances, exchanged information. He looks uncertain. She winks, playful but reassuring, and we can see her smile. The dancers repeat his line, 'I'm a blackstar.' Bowie blinks in return, perhaps making a decision, and then his face jerks out of shot. The message has been passed on, and he's gone.

'Something happened on the day he died,' the trickster announces. 'Spirit rose a metre, then stepped aside. Somebody else took his place, and bravely cried: I'm a blackstar.' 'I'm a blackstar,' the dancers answer. This was Bowie's final message to his fans, coded like the Pioneer plaque: when I die and step aside, you must take my place. When my star fades, you have to carry the torch. You must be blackstars, too. Consciously or not, they followed his instructions.

When his fellow poet Yeats died, W. H. Auden's memorial work imagined wolves 'far from his illness' continuing to race 'through the evergreen forests.' Bowie never reached the English evergreens he was running to, but his disciples did. As Auden's poem continues: 'he became his admirers'.

Soon after Bowie's death, the hashtag 'imablackstar' swept across social media; an early twenty-first-century way of paying tribute, expressing grief and connecting with others in an act of global mourning. Bowie's fans took up his message, continuing the chorus he'd begun on his final album. They gathered at impromptu shrines from Brixton to Berlin and beyond, singing 'Space Oddity' and 'Starman' together. Many of them wore hastily painted Aladdin Sane lightning bolts across their faces. Bowie had achieved his aim: making one person sound like many people, in many different contexts, in multiple spatial areas. His acolytes had come to pay tribute at all the places he'd lived around the world. In the months that followed, some adopted a more permanent mark. As one woman, @rinachan, captioned her Twitter photo of the black-star tattoo on her wrist, 'as silly as it may sound, I wanted to feel like a part of him was always still there.' His identity was dispersed among his fans; a galaxy of smaller stars who kept him alive. David Jones had passed on. Through his followers, David Bowie continued.

Of course, everything had changed. There would be no new music, barring a few posthumous tracks and recovered, remastered songs from his back catalogue. There would be no more anticipation of a new album, no surprise gifts like 'Where Are We Now?' on his birthday, no more revelations once all the secrets in the *Blackstar* artwork had been found: he left enough of those to keep us guessing for a while. We'll never see how David Bowie styled himself at age seventy-five or eighty; we'll never know how he would have redefined age, and art, for decades to come. That's an undeniable loss. 'For now,' as Visconti said, 'it is appropriate to cry.'

But in a way, nothing had changed. Very few of us ever knew David Jones, the flesh and blood man who was born in Brixton and grew up in Bromley; whose body was cremated and whose ashes were scattered in Bali. We knew 'David Bowie', the persona he created. We all have our own individual version of him, embedded in the matrix of our own lives and personal history; the meanings of his songs are unique collaborations between him and ourselves. In a sense, each of us co-created the 'David Bowie' who kept us company, consoled us and inspired us for so many years.

There's no reason for that version of Bowie to die. We can keep him with us, just like before, present in absence. We still have ~~David Bowie~~, eclipsed but radiant, and we can live up to the message of his final work by incorporating some of his energy into ourselves, following his example. He stepped aside so we could take his place and bravely cry. We can be blackstars.

How does *Lazarus* fit into this mosaic of Bowie's final work? To many critics it was a puzzle; and unlike the album *Blackstar*, and the videos for 'Blackstar' and 'Lazarus', his death didn't provide the key to its meaning. The reviews from the play's opening week, in December 2015, are full of suggestions and guesses, rather than statements. They agree that we open with Thomas Newton, played by Michael C. Hall, lying in his New York apartment, numbed by gin and starting to hallucinate. But 'has drinking really ruined him, or is it something else?' asks Kory Grow in *Rolling Stone*. 'It's hard to say.' *Lazarus* 'continually emphasizes the surreal over the explicit at nearly every turn. People splash through milk. Others pop dozens of balloons. Strange women sniff others' lingerie (frequently). Impromptu kabuki actors invade the stage.'

David Rooney, writing in the *Hollywood Reporter* on 7 December 2015, also struggles to offer a synopsis.

The extremely loose narrative jumps off from Tevis' book and Roeg's film in expanded directions. To the extent that the hallucinatory series of scenes can be boiled down (or that I understood them) the story centers on Thomas Jerome Newton (Hall), a humanoid alien who came to earth from his drought-stricken planet many years earlier. He's tormented by visions from his past and his imagination, which fuse in his memories of the blue-haired woman he loved, Mary Lou.

Other plot points can be roughly pinned down. Newton's assistant, Elly (Cristin Milioti), disguises herself as Mary Lou and separates from her husband, 'forgetting her own identity for a time', while Newton also meets an enigmatic Girl (Sophia Anne Caruso) 'sent on a mission that she initially struggles to comprehend but eventually deduces is to help Newton return to his planet'. As Rooney explains:

> But it emerges instead that it's Newton's task to help free the Girl from her limbo state, a revelation involving dark deeds related by Alan Cumming in a video insert. Finally, there are black-clad figures, led by the enigmatic Valentine (Michael Esper), who appear to be some kind of agents of death. Audiences will make more or less sense of the show depending on their willingness to invest in its unrelentingly opaque and choppy storytelling.

Ben Brantley in the *New York Times* of 7 December, also concluded his attempt at describing the plot with a disclaimer. 'This synopsis is a crude simplification, since identities are highly fluid in *Lazarus*. The script . . . switches between passages of flat-footed, literal-minded exposition and cryptic collegiate dialogue in which it's suggested that what you're seeing is only a Newton-spun illusion.' *Time Out*'s New York critic David Cote apologised if he'd summarised the story incorrectly: 'complain to the creators, who don't make *Lazarus* easy to follow. That the piece unfolds in dream logic, or as a fever dream, is fairly obvious in the first ten minutes, so best to let it wash over you without worrying about sequence or connections.'

As we saw, the video for 'Blackstar' was also met with this kind of bemused fascination; it was treated leniently as a fantasy, and criticised for its surrealistic self-indulgence. But the meaning of Bowie's final singles seemed to be unlocked after his death, their message suddenly, painfully clear. By contrast, when *Lazarus* opened in London, in November 2016, reviewers were just as baffled as their New York counterparts and, if anything, more critical. Suzannah Clapp, in the *Guardian*, acknowledged that the show 'took on a shimmering poignancy' with Bowie's death, but calls it 'long on style but short on wit . . . the script talks of rockets and flight but its vocabulary is pedestrian . . . The overall effect is not of movement but of trance.'

Stephen Dalton, reviewing the London production for the *Hollywood Reporter*, observed that the goodwill for Bowie in his homeland 'is palpable, which is handy for *Lazarus*, because this is a show which demands the indulgence of fans rather than the rigor of critics . . . reviews are likely to be as divided here as they were in New York.'

> As various characters scream, cry, die and apparently come back to life, it becomes increasingly hard to engage emotionally since nothing real seems to be at stake . . . *Lazarus* is a god-awful strange affair, perhaps because it was assembled in haste by a man who knew he was dying. But, in fairness, it does at least feel like a fitting testament to the real Bowie, who peppered his career with pretentious missteps and failed avant-garde experiments, rather than the infallible art-rock genius he has become over the past eleven months of posthumous canonization.

Dalton concludes that 'thousands of longtime fans like me will indulge him one last time in this bittersweet hometown swan song.' But when the *Guardian* asked 'what would three David Bowie fans make of *Lazarus*' − those fans also happened to be the newspaper's regular critics − the responses were just as mixed. Alexis Petridis described it as 'an incomprehensible play with wilfully stilted dialogue, in which puzzling epigrams collide with clunky exposition . . . a deeply flawed piece of work'. Hadley Freeman was disappointed by the 'impenetrable plot, absurd dialogue . . . the last half-hour is tediously po-faced'. 'It's slow. So slow,' complained Hannah Jane Parkinson. 'Few of the songs make an impact . . . why would anyone want a night out at the theatre to watch this?'

The Times gave *Lazarus* a single star, calling it 'pretentious rubbish' and 'nonsense on stilts'; the *Evening Standard* regretted that 'this isn't a mesmerising experience and it mostly feels disappointingly earthbound.' In the *Telegraph*, Dominic Cavendish captured the unexpected effect that Bowie's death had on the play. Rather than revealing its hidden meaning, it had induced a sense of obligation, transforming *Lazarus* into a 'commemorative duty' for fans, rather than a genuine pleasure. 'It feels like the height of disrespect and ingratitude to do anything other than bow low before *Lazarus*. This is David Bowie's musical-theatre epitaph.'

Can *Lazarus* be read in the same way as 'Lazarus', 'Blackstar' and *Blackstar*, the other projects that seem so clearly to consti-tute Bowie's final suite of work? There's no doubt that he was working on the play while recording *Blackstar*. He first asked to meet Enda Walsh in autumn 2014, having read all his work in advance. They embraced, and Bowie said, 'You've been in my head for three weeks.' Then, according to Chris O'Leary, 'Bowie slid four pages' worth of ideas across the table, and that was the start of it.'

'He had it mapped out for me,' Walsh recalled.

There was Thomas Jerome Newton; his savior, a dead girl; a woman ('Ellie Lazarus') 'who over this short period has a mental breakdown'; and the psychotic murderer Valentine, 'who just wants to kill fucking love!' There wouldn't be a straight narrative as much as a series of events refracted through Newton's distorted mind: the perspective of a man who can't leave earth and who can't die.

The main points on the map were there from the start, then, and they were Bowie's invention. 'Ellie Lazarus' became simply 'Elly', the original connotations of her name lost, but the rest of the plot, such as it is, was in place. Just as we assume we can read Bowie's intentions through his video collaboration with Johan Renck, so the fact that he was collaborating with Walsh, Ivo van Hove, musical director Henry Hey and the cast of *Lazarus* need not obscure Bowie's authorship. 'After Bowie became sick,' van Hove remembered, 'we had a camera installed during workshops, so he could follow. Every day, he'd call me to say: "Wow, this is great", or: "I think you should think about this." And what was a happy surprise was that he never used his power, he was collaborative. He had strong but constructive opinions.'

Clearly, he committed himself fully to the project. It was created during his illness like the *Blackstar* album, and was surely just as loaded with anxiety about his future and his legacy.

In fact, the idea of creating a musical was a more personal mission than the final album; it was the fulfilment of Bowie's lifelong dream. As we saw, *Diamond Dogs* was his substitute for a *Nineteen Eighty-Four* adaptation, but he'd originally envisioned *Ziggy Stardust* as a rock opera, and revisited that idea during the 2000s, before abandoning it. 'It just didn't come together in the way that I thought it might,' he confessed. 'The more I wrote into it, the smaller and smaller it just seemed to be.' Most recently, in 2007, he'd apparently held a series of discussions with novelist Michael Cunningham concerning a musical based around 'a stockpile of unknown, unrecorded Bob Dylan songs, which had been discovered after Dylan died. David himself would write the hitherto-unknown songs.'

Bowie had, Cunningham explained in a *GQ* article from January 2017, been 'thinking about popular artists who are not considered great artists, particularly the poet Emma Lazarus, who wrote "The New Colossus". That's the poem inscribed inside the base of the Statue of Liberty.' The conversations drifted and the project faded; and Cunningham only heard about *Lazarus* when he saw a poster outside the theatre. He emailed Bowie, who invited him to the opening night. Cunningham realised that the play 'resembled David's and my musical only in that it centered on an alien. It wasn't quite clear, at least not from the production, where the title *Lazarus* had come from, or anyway, not clear to anyone but me.'

So we know that Bowie was deeply invested in the idea of

Lazarus, that he continued to attend rehearsals despite his illness, and pushed himself to the opening night even though, according to some accounts, he was so weak he collapsed immediately after the curtain call. Ivo van Hove was one of the few people he confided in about the cancer: the director described *Lazarus* as 'something that feels very close to his heart and his head and where he's at.' It was at least as personal and as final a project as *Blackstar*. Can we understand it in those terms?

Most obviously, *Lazarus* is also about bringing things back from the archive, and modifying them into a new form to give them new life. Karaoke standards that have grown over-familiar since their original release now gain new context and resonance: Cristin Milioti invests her character's frustration into lines like 'don't tell them to grow up and out of it' from 'Changes', while 'Valentine's Day' becomes the theme song for Michael Esper's psychotic killer. This was one aspect praised by critics: David Rooney saw Hall and Caruso's performance of the usually anthemic, air-punching '"Heroes"' as 'a duet of healing deliverance', while Kory Grow recognised that 'Caruso breathes just enough drama into the cavemen and sailors of "Life on Mars" after years of overdramatic cover versions.'

Like the sorrowful call back to 'A New Career in a New Town' in 'I Can't Give Everything Away', the *Station to Station* costume in the 'Lazarus' video, the return of Major Tom in 'Blackstar', and the album's reworking of 'Sue', *Lazarus* is an adaptation of his previous work into a new form. He was closely involved with each arrangement. 'David and I sat down,' says Henry Hey about Milioti's version of 'Changes', 'and went through it section by section: start slow and pastoral, then he suggested swing.' Nicholas Pegg confirms that Bowie originally resisted '"Heroes"' as the finale, and insisted that Hey 'undercut the song's familiar setting'. According to Hey, he also 'personally approved every musician in *Lazarus*'. The house band needed to be 'all new blood'.

Even more directly and explicitly than *Blackstar*, then, *Lazarus* is a hello again and goodbye from Bowie to his back catalogue. Rather than a jukebox musical that faithfully reproduces the past, it revisits the storehouse selectively, and considers each artefact in turn. Bowie knew this would be the last time he heard those songs, and that he'd never perform them again, but he clearly wanted to shape the way they'd be heard in future. He may not have rescued 'Changes' and '"Heroes"' entirely from their status as karaoke classics, but he added another facet, giving them greater complexity and a new dimension.

Two hours with no interval may have been a long time for audiences to sit through an ambiguous fable of dreams, visions and doubles, but the play's approach to character and plot is not dissimilar to 'Lazarus' and 'Blackstar'; it's just more tolerable when it only goes on for ten minutes (though as we saw, some critics' patience was tested even by the music videos).

Like Button Eyes in 'Lazarus', Newton from *Lazarus* finishes the story where he began it, prone on the floor of the stage, staring upwards, in limbo between life and death. In the words of the theatre's artistic director James Nicola, the play is 'about choosing to live or yearning to be set free from this plane of existence'.

At the end, though, one of the wall-sized video screens shows us that the spaceship the Girl has constructed around Newton with masking tape is propelling him into outer space. From one angle at least, he's escaped; by splitting himself in two, he can find release while also remaining on earth. Van

Hove agrees that we see Hall 'still on stage alive but in his mind he is flying away into the stars', while Enda Walsh's interpretation, fittingly, offers a slightly different perspective; in his reading, Newton is 'just accepting, well, his own death at the end'. Michael C. Hall, finally, offered a third view on his character. 'Through the girl's reawakening of his vitality, Newton is brought back to life . . . that he may ready himself to die. Perhaps. Or not.'

If the three key surviving co-authors can't agree on the meaning of the final scene, perhaps we can't ever be expected to fully understand it ourselves; but the underlying ideas are clear enough. *Lazarus*, like the other parts of Bowie's final project, explores the boundary between life and death, engages with his past, and considers his legacy. Part of that legacy, as the 'Blackstar' video suggested, involved handing on his work to a younger generation. O'Leary notes that Bowie was in the business of choosing heirs, 'passing on estates, shifting properties around'. He was writing new songs, revising old ones, and handing them down. So 'Lazarus' became Hall's song, too, and he performs it live, the critics agreed, not as an impression but an adaptation of Bowie, with some of his characteristic physical gestures and vocal inflections. Hall had, in a way, become a new avatar for Bowie; a persona who would keep performing after his death.

Michael C. Hall was born in 1971, a few months before Duncan Jones. Sophia Anne Caruso was born in 2001, less than a year after Lexi Jones. The last scene of the play, before Newton either dies or soars into space, or both at once, is a duet between the two actors: the alienated protagonist and the girl he saved, or who saved him (or both at once). 'I will be king,' Newton tells her, half-joking, half believing it. 'And you . . . you will be queen.' It's a heartfelt conversation about the future between two characters the same age as Bowie's son and daughter, and the significance of that can't have escaped him. It may even have been his deliberate choice.

O'Leary observes that 'there are a wearying number of "Girls" in this play' – including a chorus of 'Teenage Girls', entirely separate from Caruso's character – but if they're Bowie's invention or co-creation, they surely say something about his state of mind and his (perhaps unconscious) priorities as the possibilities narrowed around him and his own end grew closer.

'I want Lexi to be my priority,' he'd told a journalist in June 2001. 'To spend as much time as possible with her.'

He's also conscious of growing older and being around for his daughter. 'How long have I got left?' he wonders. 'That's the saddest thing in the world, because you have this realisation that everything you love you're going to let go of and give up. I look at Lexi and think there's going to be a point when I'm not around for her. The thought of that is truly heartbreaking.'

Alexis Soloski, reviewing the original New York debut of *Lazarus*, concludes that 'it seems unlikely that it is what its collaborators imagined.' It may even, because of the pressures of time, not have been fully finished, or 'assembled in haste', as reviewer Stephen Dalton put it; Alan Cumming's role as the Girl's murderer was cut from the London production, which suggests that the play was still, to some extent, a draft in progress. Chris O'Leary comments that 'it was, among many things, a look into how Bowie's mind worked.' Perhaps that's one reason why *Lazarus* seemed hard to understand; it was an impression of his thought processes during those final months, like a sheet of paper pressed against and lifted from a whirl of coloured oils. But perhaps, too, unlike *Blackstar*, it wasn't yet meant for us. Perhaps it was also too personal for critics and fans to entirely grasp, because, on one level, *Lazarus* reads like an incomplete attempt at a letter to Lexi.

Something else happened on the day that he died. I received an email. Not to my normal account, but to one I'd set up for my research, linked to the website that featured photos from my pilgrimages, and images of me in various Bowie incarnations. Someone had found the address there and written to me. I don't remember her name – that inbox is long lost now – but she was a teenager, a Bowie fan for a few intense years, and broken-hearted about his death. She said she didn't know who else to write to, and that she didn't know if I'd reply, but she felt I'd understand. The message started 'Dear David'. She was appealing to me as an avatar.

I was still focused on the late 1990s period of his career, at the time. I'd been immersing myself in Bowie's early blog entries, his online messages to fans and his interviews about the internet. His speech and writing patterns were crowding my head: his recurring imagery, his wordplay, his playful, quizzical tone. I wrote back to her as Bowie. I didn't even have to think about the language I was choosing; it just flowed, as if I were the conduit. The email was reassuring. Yes, he'd gone on a journey, but maybe one day he'd come back. In the meantime, he was looking forward to all the new sights out there. *I don't know how efficient the postal service is going to be, where I'm headed next, but you can always drop me a line.* That kind of thing. She wrote back, thanking 'David', and saying he'd made her feel better. He'd made me feel better, too. I shut down the account soon after that. I felt it had done its job. It was time for me to move on.

And then something else happened, almost a year after he died. On his seventieth birthday, David Bowie – now a grand-father – released four new songs. Fittingly, they already felt familiar. They'd been performed and then recorded by the *Lazarus* cast, alongside the young cast's new takes on 'Changes' and '"Heroes"'; now, in a neat reversal, Bowie was putting his own spin on them. The title track, 'No Plan', was originally sung by Sophia Anne Caruso as the Girl: her version of it was clear, delicate and soaring. In Bowie's hands, it became a yearning confession and testament; finally, this was his version of 'My Way', the song he'd first attempted in 1968, and reworked as 'Life on Mars?'. But while 'My Way' is a proud, posturing look back from a man still approaching the final curtain, Bowie transforms 'No Plan' into a message from the beyond, a report on the afterlife. 'Here, there's no music here,' it begins. 'I'm lost in streams of sound. Here, am I nowhere now?'

There was a video to accompany the song, directed by Tom Hingston. Television screens glow from a shop window display at night, in shades of pale blue. A taxi passes. Streetlamps pick out raindrops on glass. The screens flicker, and begin to broadcast fragments of Bowie's transmission, one word or short phrase at a time. 'HERE'. 'I'M LOST'. A young man wearing a baseball cap pauses to watch. 'WHERE. EVER I MAY GO. JUST WHERE.' 'Just there, I am,' Bowie adds, and a bird flies across the screens.

Now there are two spectators; now three. Bowie's voice grows stronger, and more of the lyrics reach the bank of screens. 'ALL' – the word smears and distorts – 'OF THE THINGS THAT ARE MY LIFE. MY DESIRES. MY MOODS. HERE IS MY PLACE.' An aerial view of New York City, with 'Second Avenue just out of view', as the lyric puts it. A small crowd has gathered, staring into the window. 'NOTHING TO REGRET,' Bowie reflects, and the audience stares, captivated, as he shows us a shot of the earth from space. 'This is no place, but here I am,' he continues, and then broadcasts the final words, 'THIS IS NOT QUITE YET.' A quick shot of Bowie himself, from the cover of his 1993 Singles Collection, like a visual signature; then a shaky, hand-held shot of a rocket ship rising into the sky, arcing and descending. It's only a blurry glimpse, but we might recognise it as the Apollo 11 mission to the moon from July 1969, which boosted Bowie's 'Space Oddity'. We're looking back in time, right back to the start of his stardom. The screens glow briefly Mars-red, then return to blue, and the crowd has gone.

This last birthday message perfectly captures and connects the disparate strands that Bowie left unfinished, as a song from *Lazarus* is modified for a new purpose and merged with *Blackstar*, tying together loose ends. Bowie becomes Newton again – the shop is called Newton Electrical, and its multiple screens echo his bank of TVs in *The Man Who Fell to Earth* – but he also reprises the role of Major Tom, as a lost astronaut sending his last transmission back to earth. Hello again, then, to 'Space Oddity', the soundtrack to the 1969 moon mission, via 'Ashes to Ashes'. ('I've heard a rumour from Ground Control . . . oh no, don't say it's true.') One more goodbye to the guy from the early song. The idea of communicating through screens brings us back, fittingly, to *Moon* – Bowie as an artificial intelligence – and the text-to-screen dialogue is also a device in Duncan Jones's second feature, *Source Code*, where a dead man is given extra time to carry out one last mission, and takes the opportunity to phone his estranged dad.

So hello again, and goodbye, for now, to David Bowie: 'No Plan' offers him a form of immortality as an energy and voice that can return without fanfare in everyday places, speaking to everyday people, and continuing long after the death of David Jones. He continues, as 'Blackstar' suggested, through the audience that raptly receives the transmission, gathering at his glowing shrine and dispersing when the song ends. Here, though, Bowie's fans are not just young devotees but a wide range of passers-by, diverse in age and ethnicity, drawn by his presence into a temporary community. They are his fans, one year after his death; they represent all of us, carrying the torch and keeping him alive. He is present in absence, in his new form: we could refer to him now, strictly speaking, as ~~David Bowie~~, eclipsed but still glowing in the darkness.

The 'bluebird' of 'Lazarus' reappears, tinted the colour of television – 'blue, blue, electric blue', as Bowie described it in 'Sound and Vision', forty years earlier – and finally free. Images of Second Avenue, a specific reference to *Lazarus* (its theatre lies between Second Avenue and Bowery) and, more broadly, Bowie's adopted city of New York, are broadcast to a street in London, bringing him back to his home; we can tell from the street sign next to the shop, which reads Foxgrove Road. That was his address with Mary Finnigan in Beckenham in 1969; the flat where he wrote 'Space Oddity'. But the location isn't really Foxgrove Road. The sign has been changed.

Bowie's final video was shot in a disguised launderette on Endwell Road, in Brockley, south-east London. You can still see the painted advertisement on the wall, next to the fake electrical shop. 'For all your cleaning needs, open seven days a week.' I recognised it instantly. That was my road, from 2000 to 2007, and I walked past the launderette almost every day.

Of course, it was coincidence. It couldn't possibly have been deliberate in any way. But in this case, I didn't care about the logic behind it, and simply embraced the uncanny sense of fate. I'd spent a year immersed in Bowie's life, visiting all his old haunts from Brixton to Bromley, Beckenham to

Berlin, Lausanne to New York City, and now, finally, on his seventieth birthday, he'd come home to me. It had ended well. It was the perfect ending to a chapter in my life.

David Bowie, of course, would continue.

CONCLUSION:
DAVID BOWIE – A LEGACY

Where are we now? Where is he now? Still present in absence; still there, appearing in unexpected places and strange disguises, like a spirit briefly inhabiting and animating the people he left behind, then passing on. In 2016, the Disney animation *Moana* featured a song that could have been written by an alternate Bowie in his glam rock period: Lin-Manuel Miranda composed it for Jemaine Clement, who'd already spoofed Bowie's cockney vibrato in *Flight of the Conchords*. 'Watch me dazzle like a diamond in the rough . . . strut my stuff.' Online impressionist Stevie Riks completed the connection by performing a full-blown Bowie version of the Disney track, claiming it was a lost recording.

Genuine lost recordings surface again too, alongside re-releases of old tracks. July 2018 saw the announcement that *Never Let Me Down*, perhaps Bowie's weakest album, had been entirely remastered – stripped down to the vocals, then rebuilt with new drums, guitar and bass tracks. 'Sometimes posthumous projects are tricky,' said composer Nico Muhly. 'But in a way, knowing that the band and the ecosystem continues without him is actually really quite beautiful.' Days later, Bowie was in the news again: David Hadfield, former drummer of The Konrads, had discovered their long-lost demo of 'I Never Dreamed' in a breadbasket. It sold for £32,000 at auction. At the other end of his career, the track thought to be Bowie's final *Blackstar* recording, 'Blaze' – described by Nicholas Pegg, one of the few to have heard it, as optimistic, aspirational and joyful – is still held in limbo, waiting for an official release. In the meantime, we have to make do with his avatars and impersonators.

In May 2017, Gillian Anderson channelled the 'Life on Mars?' Bowie in the TV adaptation of Neil Gaiman's *American Gods*, adopting a south London accent and Bowie's slight, hissy lisp as she lectured a younger deity. 'You've got your transmission and your live wire. But your circuit's dead. Take a look at you. Beating up the wrong guy.' Cate Blanchett wore a version of the ice-blue 'Life on Mars?' suit in *Ocean's 8*, in summer 2018, emphasising the androgyny of Bowie's early image. As Kate Moss showed back in 2003, with a

Vogue shoot in his iconic outfits, and Iselin Steiro confirmed in 2013's 'The Stars (Are Out Tonight)' video, it takes a slim, sleek woman to play Bowie as a young man.

Bowie's voice also returned from the imaginary archive – performed by male actors – in two radio plays. *The Final Take*, written by David Morley and broadcast in January 2018, had comedian Jon Culshaw toning down his usual exaggerated impressions into a more sober, hesitant tribute of Bowie in the Blackstar studio. Another BBC drama, *Low* (July 2018) revisited the Berlin years: Daniel Weyman played Bowie broadly, in a satirical approximation. Clearly the later years are still off-limits to anything but the most respectful treatment, but the mid-seventies are fair game; on radio, at least. Duncan Jones greeted the news of a new Bowie movie, *Stardust*, with fierce dismissal. 'Pretty sure nobody has been granted music rights for any biopic . . . I would know.' He wryly suggested he'd only approve an animated film about his dad's characters, scripted by Gaiman and directed by the creators of *Spider-Man: Into The Spider-Verse*. Jones's own tributes to his father have been small-scale and subtle: a dedication at the end of the 2018 Netflix feature *Mute*, which incorporated Philip Glass's version of '"Heroes"', and thoughtful tweets around key anniversaries, sharing his personal reflections with the broader community of Bowie fans.

On stage, a recording of Rob Newman as Bowie continued to talk to Martin (played by Alex Walton), the troubled young fan of Adrian Berry's *From Ibiza to the Norfolk Broads*, which opened in October 2016 and toured for the next sixteen months. Here, Bowie is a disembodied but constant companion, his deep tones always reassuring; Rob Newman's script is taken from interviews, up to the point where he speaks directly to the protagonist. Again, with Bowie gone, we are left imagining what he might have said, and inventing new lines, new scenes, even new songs for him in his absence.

Of course, 'Blackstar' wasn't the last we heard of Major Tom. Bowie might have given the spaceman his last sign-off, but even in the 1969 lyric Tom became public property ('the papers want to know whose shirts you wear'), and now floats throughout popular culture. He was brought back by Luc Besson in 2017 as the soundtrack to *Valerian's* opening sequence of galactic exploration and alien contact, and in February 2018, Elon Musk sent the song out into space, as one of the tracks playing on his Tesla Roadster sports car. The crash dummy driver, which Musk called 'Starman', now orbits the sun in a real-world echo of Tom's fate in the 'Blackstar' video.

As we saw in the first chapter, Bowie's death prompted cartoons, memes and tweets about his return to his original, astral home. By summer, another half-serious theory was circulating about Bowie's role as the stable centre of world affairs, or, in the words of actor Paul Bettany on Twitter, 'the glue holding the universe together'. 'Reality Continues to

Crumble in the Wake of David Bowie's Death', *NewsThump* reported in July 2016. The article was tongue-in-cheek, of course, but the sentiment was genuine: as one fan plaintively put it, faced with the news of further celebrity deaths and terrorist attacks across Europe, 'The world has just fallen to pieces ever since David Bowie died, hasn't it really.'

In July 2018, Bowie was invoked again, in the context of a sealed sarcophagus discovered in Alexandria. 'They open the mysterious black sarcophagus,' proposed @iucounu in a message that earned 17,000 likes, 'and inside it's David Bowie, alive and well. He then sets about repairing the timeline using the occult knowledge he won through trickery in the under-world.' In his absence, after his passing, David Bowie has been – jokingly, but perhaps not entirely jokingly – reimagined as a modern god.

His hardcore fans, as we'd expect, keep the spark and the spirit alive. In Berlin during 2017 and 2018, a performer with the pseudonym Crayon Jones adopted a second persona, Iggy Stardust, in a glam rock musical, *Loving the Alien*: 'a story of love, sex, loneliness, betrayal, family and the galactic apoca-lypse'. In Britain, Andy Jones and Nick Smart are working on the latest issue of *David Bowie: Glamour*, a lavishly glossy zine designed by Lizzie Capewell with painted covers by Helen Green, praised by *GQ* as one of its '100 best things in the world 2018'. In Brooklyn, the *David Bowie Is* exhibition continued until June 2018, with a gallery showcasing fan art;

this was the exhibition's final stop on its five-year world tour, but it was revived as an interactive phone app in spring of the following year. Bowie was an early adopter of the internet, predicting its 'unimaginable' cultural influence in a Jeremy Paxman interview from 1999, which went viral after his death. It was eerily fitting that the archive of his life would be preserved in an alternate reality.

Bowie's music is, of course, still performed live. Bruce Springsteen, returning the favour of Bowie's 'Hard to Be a Saint in the City' and 'Growin' Up' from the *Pin Ups* period, covered 'Rebel Rebel' in January 2016; weeks later Michael Stipe, echoing Nirvana's *Unplugged* performance, sang a stripped-down 'Man Who Sold the World' on *The Tonight Show*. At a March 2016 concert in Toronto, Prince segued from a simple, piano version of his own 'Dolphin' into Bowie's '"Heroes"', less than a month before his own death. Lorde stepped out, wearing a Thin White Duke-style white shirt and black waistcoat, to fill the empty gap on stage at the 2016 Brit Awards. She was one of Bowie's chosen heirs – he'd generously described her as the 'future of music' – and an appropriate choice to serve as his avatar, in his absence.

Tribute acts continue, too, their performances now a cele-bration of the past rather than an impersonation of a living legend. In the UK alone, fans can follow The BowieXperience, Absolute Bowie, Ultimate Bowie, Aladdinsane, David Live and my old band, the Thin White Duke. At the more elite and expensive level, Bowie 'alumni' are still touring, their core members supplemented by special guests: 'A Bowie Celebration' is led by pianist Mike Garson with lead guitarist Earl Slick, while drummer Woody Woodmansey and bassist/producer Tony Visconti head Holy Holy. 'We're not a tribute band,' proclaims Visconti on the website, 'we are the real deal!' The 'Bowie Celebration' site makes a similar, competing claim: 'It's not a cover band. It's the actual band. It's as close as you're going to get to Bowie.' In his absence, we are offered a second-hand connection with the star through his former associates. Bowie might have raised an eyebrow to see his bandmates quibbling, years after his death, about which of them offers the most authentic experience.

At the time of writing, Tony Visconti and Mike Garson are in their seventies; Woody Woodmansey and Earl Slick are in, or approaching, their late sixties. I've been to those tribute gigs, from the amateur to the elite, and found myself surrounded by people older than me. In my head, Bowie still speaks to the thirteen-year-old who first discovered 'Ricochet' on *Let's Dance*, but seeing his music performed live now brings the uncomfortable truth home that his bandmates are all of retirement age, and his most loyal fanbase only a decade or so younger. And if you do the maths, it's no surprise. Bowie was born in 1947. An eighteen-year-old today would have been born at the very start of the 2000s. The gap is roughly equivalent to me – born in 1970 – immersing myself, as an adolescent, in the music of Frank Sinatra, Billie Holiday or Edith Piaf, all born in 1915: not inconceivable, but perhaps unusual. Bowie is two generations apart from today's teenagers. Will his legacy age with the fans who followed him in their own teens, during the 1970s and 1980s, and pass on with them? Bowie is kept alive now by people who grew up with him, as I did. But where will he be in 2050?

Bowie first attended Bromley Technical School in September 1958, catching the number 410 bus with George Underwood. I took an Uber from Bromley South Station, in June 2018. In the foyer of the main reception – Bromley Tech is now Ravens Wood School, but the building is fundamentally unchanged – I waited under the staircase where Bowie used to jam with Peter Frampton. Underwood remembered joining in. 'I'd be playing guitar and David would sing. We did Buddy Holly and Everly Brothers stuff. He was a good harmoniser.'

Elizabeth Potter-Hicks, head of music, led me up those stairs, past a mural of Bowie, to a classroom with a drum kit at the centre and instruments leaning against the walls. She introduced me to a group of her students from the sixth form music academy. This was their tutor room, their territory, and they were comfortable here, lounging and chatting. They were mostly young men, buzzing with end-of-term enthusiasm but polite and respectful, and still wearing a modified version of uniform, including ties and blazers. In the middle of our conversation, three of their friends burst in, freed from their final exam: they toured the room for high fives and handshakes, apologising cheerfully to me. Two young women dipped coolly in and out of the discussion. When these students were born, Bowie was fifty-four, and working on his twenty-second studio album, *Heathen*; he was just a few years from the heart problems that would push him towards a quiet semi-retirement in New York. I wanted to know what he meant to them – whether he meant anything at all – and how they thought he'd be remembered.

They all knew about him, of course, because of the media attention after his death. Newspapers and television crew had turned up at Ravens Wood on 11 January, looking for a new angle. Some of the students had been studying 'Space Oddity', and performed it live for the cameras, for the first time and with very little preparation. 'They really got inside it,' Elizabeth confirmed. For George Hunt, that was his introduction to Bowie, at age fifteen. It took Bowie's death to prompt public recollections of his life, and to bring his past to George's teenage attention.

Others had learned about Bowie when they first joined the school, which is proud of its role in his history. There's another portrait of him in the main hall, next to Hanif Kureishi, who attended Ravens Wood a generation later, and music students in particular are soon given a crash course in his work. Zander Solis hadn't heard of Bowie until he joined the music academy. 'Then we started performing some of his songs, and I thought they were really upbeat,' he offered helpfully. 'Really nice to listen to.'

I wondered how Bowie would have felt, being described as 'nice' after putting so much effort into subverting binaries, pushing boundaries and experimenting with styles and genres. I asked Zander what songs he'd first played. 'Let's Dance', he told me, and 'Modern Love'; the same album I'd been captivated by in 1983. They'd recorded a cover version, and talked me through it with intelligent awareness of technique, arrangement and production, right down to the positioning of the woodblocks in the stereo mix. As Elizabeth had said, they were deep inside the music, though their route was different from mine as a teenager focused more on English literature. Someone shouted across the room that they'd done 'Starman' too, and they began singing the chorus. I joined in. They didn't stop immediately, or laugh. Maybe Zander had chosen the right word after all. It was nice.

Some of them had been introduced to Bowie by parents, or teachers. Ellora Kowalczyk – she hesitated before telling me her surname, knowing I'd struggle to spell it – told me about her Year Six tutor, when she was eleven. 'It was just some stupid English task,' she recalled with offhand contempt. 'We had to, like, write about going into space or something, and he was obsessed with Bowie, and put on "Space Oddity" or something. I don't really remember, it was a while ago, but that was the first time I listened to him.' Her tone became a little more generous. 'That was when I got into him.'

Alex Getting had a similar experience with his dad, who had attended Ravens Wood in the eighties.

He had a massive sense of pride that he'd gone to the same school as David Bowie, and that was probably a big reason why he pushed me to go to this school too. He introduced me to lots of his songs. I definitely would say I like them, but they're not exactly my favourite songs ever. I mean, I respect him, I appreciate old music, and his music's good, but I wouldn't necessarily say . . .

He laughed. 'It wouldn't be on my playlist.'

Joe Spiteri's mum was a 'big fan . . . she really pushed him onto me and she's given me his records as well. She saw him live a couple of times.' His experience was similar to mine, three decades earlier, but with CDs instead of cassettes. 'From a really young age, when we used to go on holidays, she used to play Bowie in the car on CDs, and we'd just listen to them, and get to know him. And then I started liking him, and she told me he went here . . . and I was set on going to this school.'

The first tracks he remembers are 'Changes' and 'Life on Mars?' from a compilation album. 'But all the songs just seemed to . . . sound good to me,' he explained, trying to find the right words.

Zander interrupted. 'Timeless.'

At my own university, as I described in a previous chapter, a young man had exploded with frustration at Bowie's appropriation of gay culture and identity. I told the Ravens Wood students about him. They were more forgiving. 'I think Bowie actually did more socially than musically,' Ellora suggested.

Like I feel he's done so much, especially for the gay community, with the whole idea of having different genders. I feel he kind of started it . . . of course, he didn't start it, as people had felt like that before, but he brought it to light more, and influenced people. Even now, people don't really get the idea of switching genders, and I feel that Bowie, through his different characters and stuff, portrayed that . . . not being exactly male or female. In the eighties there was a trend where all the males wore make-up. He must have influenced that.

'Good times!' I added, remembering my own adolescence. She ignored me.

Another young man, Sean Kenny, joined the discussion. 'I think in doing that, he might have been emulating drag queens, and drag was heavily, heavily linked with gay rights, with things like Stonewall.'

Could they see an argument that he was borrowing a minority group's culture and using it for his own ends?

'Isn't that the whole cultural appreciation and appropriation thing?' Ellora replied, warming to her theme. 'I've been having long debates on this, as someone from like, lots of different ethnicities. Basically, I've decided it's only appropriation if you don't appreciate a culture. And I feel like he did, he really appreciated the gay culture, he really kind of understood it, and so therefore he helped it along. It's not like he stole it or anything.'

George remembered the anecdote about Bowie wearing his 'man's dress' on an American tour. He knew the story in impressive detail.

The album hadn't been released yet, and he went around the Deep South, wearing a dress, just because! And a man pulled a gun on him and said, 'What do you think you're doing?' And Bowie just stood there and said, 'I think I look beautiful.' And he just walked away, and the man was stumped. I think if he was just taking the mick out of it, he wouldn't have done that. He must have been confident in what he was doing and what he was representing, just to walk round . . .

'But he's gone back on a lot of that,' Sean countered.

I think he was at heart an experimentalist, and wanted to just try everything out. So he said let's bring in these bits of gay culture, let's bring in these bits of black culture, let's bring in all of this, and on the one hand, you could see it as appropriation or just demeaning those cultures, but on the other, I think he was just interested to see what everything had to offer.

Ellora picked up on the idea of racial appropriation, with reference to Bowie's mid-seventies soul period. 'But the fact is, he did actually go to Philadelphia. It's not like he was mocking them and just using their drum patterns, he actually went there, learned about them, spent time with them, and then he used it.'

'He did the work,' I suggested.

'Exactly. That's like, completely acceptable. He's bringing it all in.'

'It's hard to know whether he meant everything he said,' George added. 'In his interviews, it was hard to tell which part of him was the caricature, and which one was actually David Bowie. Especially during the, um . . . the Thin White Priest, or whatever.' Laughter. I assured him that Thin White Priest would have been a great stage name. 'It was very hard,' George went on, correcting himself. 'Hard to tell which of his statements were the Duke, and which ones were him.'

Was Bowie wrong to go back on his earlier statements that he was gay or bisexual? George considered. 'I think it was wrong of him to say it's a mistake. It would be better to say, that's who I was then, and I've changed as a person. By saying it was a mistake, it implies it was a bad thing. It's a mistake to get drunk and do something stupid. It's not a mistake to be one thing and then decide you don't . . .' – he paused, then found the right phrase – 'identify with that any more.'

They were unimpressed by the idea of Bowie's former band-mates touring. 'I think concerts like that probably appeal to people who grew up with Bowie, rather than younger people who like him nowadays,' said Sean. George suggested that Bowie's future was online, through platforms like YouTube, rather than tribute gigs. 'Instead of seeing other musicians play live, people can actually watch the Bowie play live' – he used the definite article – 'in gigs from twenty or thirty years ago. And now you'll get covers, or songs inspired by him.'

Joe agreed:

People might find his songs on a playlist, not know where it's from, and incorporate it into their own music. His abstract sounds could be used in another song, and then people who don't know Bowie will find themselves listening to him. You'll get more remixes, and the families of people who heard the songs will play them to their children, down the line.

Would they introduce their own children to Bowie's music, in future? A chorus of 'definitely'. 'But not, like, throw it at them,' Zander added. 'I think more in the same way that Joe's known Bowie through his parents playing it when he was little.'

How would Bowie be remembered? Sean suggested a historical perspective: 'The further you go back in history, the less musicians there are that stick, until you go back to classical composers and you have one every ten, twenty years. But I think he'll be one of those people that will still be played and still be remembered for quite a long time, even if it's more as an oldie, and your grandparents' music.'

They recognised that they were unusual, as music students at Bowie's former school. I asked what their other friends thought of him. Sean put on a slow, stupid voice. 'They're like, is he the one with lightning on his face? The really weird guy?'

'They know he had different coloured eyes,' said Joe. 'And they remember "Changes" because it was in *Shrek*.' They all laughed.

'What they know about Bowie is basically that he was really weird, as a person,' Sean explained.

Joe, the long-term fan, sounded wearily frustrated. 'If they'd just sit down and take the time to research about why he did the things he did, about the background behind the songs, then they'd understand.'

'He'll be remembered by most people as a symbol, like Elvis,' George proposed. 'A few quotes, a face, a name, a person from history. And they'll remember what he did for the gay cultures. Maybe in thirty years there'll be a trend for Bowie-esque songs, or hipsters who rediscover him. He'll be remembered in a niche kind of way, by people who listen to old music.'

'He might just be a name,' said Joe pessimistically.

'I think he'll definitely be sampled, by people who appreciate him,' George assured him. 'People will still hear David Bowie, but through different voices, so they won't necessarily know who it is.'

Will people still listen to songs like 'Let's Dance'? Zander piped up: 'I'll be listening!' More laughter. And then Joe Spiteri half raised his hand, politely asking permission. They were quiet while he spoke, looking round at them all, his voice deep and deliberate. It struck me that he even looked like Bowie at seventeen: earnest and clean-cut, with his hair, jacket and tie neatly styled, but with a controlled intensity in his eyes.

'He will still be the amazing musician we all know,' Joe began. 'His music . . . it's all about memories. You remember the first time you heard one song. You remember that you were on holiday, and the good times you had. You remember specific moments that were important to you. And those moments . . . were Bowie's songs.'

We were all silent. His classmates nodded. I kept recording. There were murmurs and smiles, and then I stood up and said, 'Well, I think we've got it.' Joe Spiteri, aged seventeen, had just summed up in a few lines why David Bowie matters.

ACKNOWLEDGEMENTS

Thanks to Tom Killingbeck, my editor at William Collins, and Veronique Baxter, my agent at David Higham; and thanks to Roger Bacardy and Nick Smart for their expert feedback.

This book is dedicated to Ethan Jack Brooker, who was born between chapters one and two: my absolute beginner.

DAVID BOWIE'S DISCOGRAPHY

1967
David Bowie

1969
David Bowie, also known as *Man of Words/Man of Music*, and re-released as *Space Oddity*

1970
The Man Who Sold The World

1971
Hunky Dory

1984
Tonight

1983
Let's Dance

1980
Scary Monsters (And Super Creeps)

1979
Lodger

1987
Never Let Me Down

1989
Tin Machine

1991
Tin Machine II

1993
Black Tie White Noise

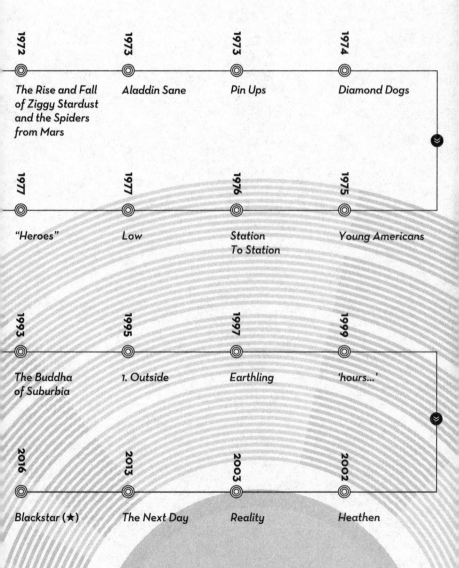

BIBLIOGRAPHY

Bakhtin, M. 1982. Trans. Holquist, M. and Emerson, C. The Dialogic Imagination: Four Essays. Texas: University of Texas Press.

Bengry, J. 2013. 'Films and Filming: The Making of a Queer Marketplace in Pre-Decriminalization Britain'. Lewis, B. (Ed.) British Queer History: New Approaches and Perspectives. Manchester: Manchester University Press, 244-266.

Bowie, A. with Carr, P. 1993. Backstage Passes: Life on the Wild Side With David Bowie. New York: G.P. Putnam's Sons.

Brooker, W. Forever Stardust: David Bowie Across The Universe. London: I B Tauris.

Buckley, D. 2005. Strange Fascination: David Bowie: The Definitive Story. London: Virgin Books

Cann, K. 2012. Any Day Now: David Bowie The London Years: 1947-1974. Croydon: Adelita

Collis, C. 2002. 'Feeling My Age'. Blender, August.

Critchley, S. 2016. On Bowie. London: Serpents Tail.

Crowe, C. 1976. 'Ground Control to Davy Jones'. Rolling Stone, February 12.

Crowe, C. 1976. 'Playboy Interview: David Bowie'. Playboy, September.

David, H. 1998. On Queer Street: A Social History of British Homosexuality, 1895-1995. London: HarperCollins.

Deleuze, G. and Guattari, F. 2004. Trans. Massumi, B. A Thousand Plateaus: Capitalism and Schizophrenia. London: Continuum.

Derrida, J. 1961. Trans. Johnson. B. Dissemination. Chicago: University of Chicago Press.

Derrida, J. 1976. Trans. Spivak, G. C. Of Grammatology. London and Baltimore: John Hopkins University Press.

Devereux, E., Dillane, A. and Power, M. (Eds.) 2015. David Bowie: Critical Perspectives. London: Routledge.

Doggett, P. 2011. The Man Who Sold The World: David Bowie and the 1970s. London: Bodley Head.

Dyer, R. 2002. The Culture Of Queers. London: Routledge.

Egan, S. (Ed.) 2015. Bowie on Bowie: Interviews & Encounters. London: Souvenir Press.

Gill, J. 1995. Queer Noises. Minneapolis: University of Minnesota Press.

Gillman, P. and Gillman, L. 1986. Alias David Bowie: A Biography. London: Hodder and Stoughton.

Greco, N. P. 2015. David Bowie in Darkness: A Study of 1. Outside and the Late Career. North Carolina: McFarland.

Hewitt, P. 2012. Bowie: Album By Album. Bath: Palazzo Editions.

Hughes, T. 1970. 'Bowie For A Song'. Jeremy, January.

Leigh, W. 2014. Bowie: The Biography. New York: Gallery Books.

Jameson, F. 1992. Postmodernism: Or, the Cultural Logic of Late Capitalism. London: Verso.

Jones, D. 2012. When Ziggy Played Guitar: David Bowie and Four Minutes That Shook The World. London: Preface.

Jones, D. 2017. David Bowie: A Life. London: Preface.

Loder, K. 1983. 'Straight Time'. Rolling Stone, May 12.

Mendelssohn, J. 1971. 'David Bowie: Pantomime Rock?' Rolling Stone, April 1.

O'Leary, C. 2015. Rebel Rebel. Hants: Zero Books.

O'Leary, C. 2019. Ashes to Ashes. London: Repeater Books.

Pegg, N. 2016. The Complete David Bowie. London: Titan.

Plitnick, M. 2013. 'We Can Be Heroes'. Souciant, 3 May. http://souciant.com/2013/05/we-can-be-heroes/.

Raphael, L. 2006. 'Betrayed by David Bowie'. Secret Anniversaries of the Heart. Massachusetts: Leapfrog Press.

Reynolds, S. 2016. Shock and Awe: Glam Rock and Its Legacy, from the Seventies to the Twenty-First Century. New York: HarperCollins.

Sandford, C. Bowie: Loving the Alien. New York: Da Capo.

Spitz, M. 2010. Bowie: A Biography. London: Aurum Press.

Stark, T. (2016) 'Confronting Bowie's Mysterious Corpses'. Cinque, T., Moore, C. and Redmond, S. (Eds.) Enchanting David Bowie: Space/Time/Body/Memory. London: Bloomsbury, 61-77.

Thomson, E. and Gutman, D. (Eds.) 1995. The Bowie Companion. London: Macmillan.

Tremlett, G. 1997. David Bowie: Living on the Brink. New York: Carroll & Graf.

Trynka, P. 2011. Starman: David Bowie - The Definitive Biography. London: Sphere

Turner, V. 1990. 'Are There Universals of Performance in Myth, Ritual and Drama?' Schechner, W. and Appels. W. (Eds.) By Means of Performance: Intercultural Studies of Theatre and Ritual. New York: Cambridge University Press.

Turner, V. 1997. The Ritual Process. New York: Aldine de Gruyter.

Vermorel, F, and J. 1985. Starlust: The Secret Fantasies of Fans. London: W.H. Allen.

Watts, M. 1972. 'Oh You Pretty Thing'. Melody Maker, January 22.

INDEX